THE FISHMONGER'S
APPRENTICE

QUARRY

QUARRY BOOKS

BOOKS

BEVERLY MASSACHUSETTS

THE EXPERT'S GUIDE TO
SELECTING, PREPARING, AND
COOKING A WORLD
OF SEAFOOD, TAUGHT BY THE
MASTERS

WITH PHOTOGRAPHY
BY STEVE LEGATO

THE FISHMONGER'S APPRENTICE ALIZA GREEN

First published in the United States of America by
Quarry Books, a member of
Quayside Publishing Group
100 Cummings Center
Suite 406-L
Beverly, Massachusetts 01915-6101
Telephone: (978) 282-9590
Fax: (978) 283-2742
www.quarrybooks.com

Library of Congress Cataloging-in-Publication Data

Green, Aliza.
  Fishmonger's apprentice : the expert's guide to selecting, preparing, and cooking a world of seafood, taught by the masters / Aliza Green.
    p. cm.
  Includes bibliographical references and index.
  ISBN-13: 978-1-59253-653-5
  ISBN-10: 1-59253-653-0
  1. Cooking (Fish) 2. Cooking (Seafood) I. Title.
  TX747.G785 2010
  641.6'92—dc22
                              2010029009

ISBN-13: 978-1-59253-653-5
ISBN-10: 1-59253-653-0

10 9 8 7 6 5 4 3 2 1

Design: Paul Burgess: Burge Agency
Artwork: Peter Usher: Burge Agency
Photography: Steve Legato, except for the following:
    Page 8: Dominic Episcopo
    Page 26: Felicia Perretti
    Page 34: Salumeria Rosi
    Page 42: Giorgio Zajotti
    Page 60: Dr. John Kaneko and the
            Hawaii Seafood Council
    Page 72: Lance Forman
    Page 88: Marco Santini
    Pages 92 and 94: Jimmy Phillips
    Page 102: Nick Clayton
    Page 105: Cleanseas
    Page 121: Elyse Brown
    Page 126: Michael McNicholas
    Page 130: Barry O'Toole, courtesy of the
            Fishmongers' Company
    Page 136: Manu Bastien
    Page 162: Sheila Holland-Dassatt
    Pages 182 and 183: Simon Desrochers
    Pages 190 and 192: Eric Stabach

Printed in China

TO THE COURAGEOUS AND DEDICATED FISHING FAMILIES OF THE WORLD.

CONTENTS

INTERVIEWS WITH THE MASTERS

ILLUSTRATED TECHNIQUES

SAMUEL D'ANGELO, INDUSTRY ADVISOR FOR THIS BOOK, IS A FOURTH-GENERATION SEAFOOD EXPERT WHO BUILT A CORNER STORE INTO A LARGE AND RESPECTED WHOLESALER BASED IN PHILADELPHIA AND SERVING RESTAURANTS AND RETAILERS FROM NEW YORK TO WASHINGTON, D.C.

FOREWORD

My grandparents, all born in Sicily, instilled in their children the culture of the sea and the way to sustain our living from it. As a young man, I would travel to Sicily with my grandfather and visit local fish markets. The catch of the day might be just a half dozen small fish including perhaps a few small whiting, which not long before had been abundant and cheap. Back in Philadelphia, I'd see the large king whiting we'd get from Maine. Now those big whiting are essentially gone except for in Alaska, which has a sustainable fishery. Unfortunately, what I saw in Europe close to forty years ago is happening in many places now. Because of what I learned, Samuels & Son is committed to being known as *the* sustainable fish supplier in the region as part of our investment in the strong future of our fisheries, oceans, and waterways.

When you grow up in a fish market, you learn the many ways of the seafood world—the skills and knowledge garnered by generations of fishermen and fishmongers. My grandfather, Giuseppe Ippolito, started out peddling fish on the street. Later he got a horse and cart, then a truck, and eventually a corner store, Ippolito's, which our family still owns and operates. My mother, Rose D'Angelo was the original fishmonger. She could cut and fillet any fish my grandfather Giuseppe brought her. I learned the trade in my free time. Daily, I practiced cutting and filleting, weighing and wrapping, and finishing the sale by ringing it up at the register. It was more than a corner store for me, it was our family's foundation.

When Christmas came, I couldn't wait to work in the store with all my cousins. We all had our chores: One scrubbed the walls and floors, another cleaned the basement where we soaked our bacala and stockfish, and a third took out the guts and fish heads to the barrels destined for pig fodder for nearby farms. On Christmas Eve, we all sat at the table and feasted together on the traditional seven fishes—or more.

The 1970s brought a renaissance in food, and the fish followed. Our business wasn't just for the neighborhood anymore. We began selling to local restaurants and taprooms. Mussel and clam consumption was going up and fish such as red snapper and wild salmon became a staple for us. In 1974, after graduating from Central High school, I became the buyer, running the whole operation. I just loved working with this stuff!

In 1989, I opened our wholesale company because our restaurant trade had grown considerably. We took all our knowledge and perseverance and basically went to battle with our competition—companies that just a short time ago were our suppliers. As a small wholesaler, we didn't have a strong relationship yet with our vendors, so sourcing was a constant challenge. But we never relented and came through for our customers with some of the nicest and freshest seafood ever brought into Philadelphia. By 1995, Samuels had grown to a solid distributor and we were ready to send our seafood to other cities.

In 2009, we moved into new efficient green headquarters and started our own Sustained Seas Program, becoming the only MSC-certified fish company in the region. (The Marine Stewardship Council, a global organization started in the United Kingdom, works with fisheries, seafood companies, scientists, conservation groups, and the public to promote the best environmental choices in seafood through its fishery certification program.) We are now a major regional distributor, importing fish and shellfish from around the world.

It's so important to educate consumers. If people don't trust their fishmonger, they'll buy only for price. You can't do that with fresh fish. It all goes back to the fishmonger—the person working behind the counter. Fishmongers are special, they watch out for us and all the creatures they live and work with. If they don't know what they're doing, they're not going to be able to sell something new. The average consumer has very little idea about what they're buying. Unless the fishmonger can explain how to cook it, people won't touch an unfamiliar fish. Most people eat a limited variety of fish. In my childhood, mackerel, bluefish, porgy, butterfish, and sardines were staples. I still keep a can of mackerel around for a quick lunch. Herring has unbelievable flavor and nutritional benefits. I'd like to see more people expand their seafood repertoires to some of these underutilized—and delicious—species.

The seafood business is as hard as ever. I don't think that will ever change, but I still love to handle the fish. We work every day at Samuels as a family. My four children work with me and the grandchildren come and visit. All of us need to be aware and act appropriately to preserve the bounties of the sea so that our grandchildren have the same opportunity as I did growing up, to enjoy and work with the fish and shellfish from our oceans and rivers.

CHOOSING THE BEST SEAFOOD

Fish tastes its best when it's in season and plentiful.

The time to buy fish is when the price is low; the time to eat it is right away.

Use your eyes, your nose, and if permitted, your hands to choose that fish, using tips in this book. Most important, buy from someone who knows and cares.

Be flexible: Buy the best looking fish, not necessarily the one you came in for. Many fish can be easily substituted: for example, black sea bass, striped bass, red snapper, yellowtail snapper, and hybrid striped bass will all work for the same dish.

Individually line-caught (or trolling) fish is generally of higher quality than net-caught. Fish that is caught, promptly bled, and immediately chilled is best.

Venture into ethnic markets to get a different selection of seafood and often at a lower price than mainstream markets.

Try less sought-after species such as porgies, weakfish, or croakers, which may be bony, darker-fleshed species such as bluefish, mahimahi, or mackerel, or uncommon species such as skate, which are usually sauteed, and red gurnard, which are excellent in soup.

INTRODUCTION

Once everyone shopped at the local butcher's shop, bakery, and fishmonger (often combined with the greengrocer). Today, most people shop in supermarkets, although direct sales through farmer's markets are increasing every year. Some farmer's markets even have fishmongers. Shoppers at farmer's market can buy everything from local oysters to hard-shell clams and frozen halibut cheeks. Many thriving specialty fish markets are multiple-generation family businesses. Fish markets close to port (freshwater or saltwater) usually specialize in local seafood.

A monger is a dealer in a specific commodity. A fishmonger sells fish, a coster-monger sells fruits and vegetables, and an ironmonger sells things made from iron. Fishmongering is a venerable term that derives from as far back as thirteenth-century London.

The definitions of the words fish and seafood are murky. The first Merriam-Webster's definition for fish is, "an aquatic animal—usually used in combination like starfish and cuttlefish," which means that fish is also seafood ("edible marine fish and shellfish"). In this book, I have divided the harvest of the water into fish and seafood, itself divided into mollusks, crustaceans, and echinoderms (sea urchins in this book).

In *The Fishmonger's Apprentice*, I have surveyed the world of fish and seafood so that you can make thoughtful, environmentally, and nutritionally conscious choices. The diverse interviews, comprehensive instructions, and photos so fresh you lose that "fear of seafood" will help you gain the confidence to enjoy choosing, storing, preparing, cooking, eating, and perhaps catching the delicious bounty of our waters.

I've interviewed experts, from fishermen and -women to aqua farmers, fish smokers, seafood wholesalers, and chefs around the world because the seafood business is truly global. A single species of swordfish swims the globe. One species of bluefin tuna swims the northern hemisphere; a second swims the southern hemisphere. The choices we make affect our planet and the lives of people everywhere.

In recent decades, there have been titanic changes in the seafood industry: availability, environmental concerns, challenges to international fishing stocks, the spectacular growth of aqua-farming, and techno-logical advances. Advances in freezing technology that allow fish to be flash-frozen often on board a ship have greatly improved quality. Advances in packaging protect frozen seafood by keeping the oxygen out.

ENVIRONMENTAL CONCERNS AND HAZARDS

With our oceans and freshwater sources becoming depleted of once-abundant fish, making good choices is crucial to the future of our planet's ecosystem.

Mercury is a health concern, especially from larger predator fish at the top of the food chain. Despite this, eating fish has great health benefits, which can be maximized by consuming a variety of seafood. So, eat lots of different kinds of seafood, not too much of one kind; and try something you've never eaten before.

Our oceans are the home to thousands of marine species, so it is important to keep them clean and safe. Many coastal wetlands have been polluted and ocean floors have been severely damaged by fishing nets and dragging. Whenever possible, buy fish caught using fishing methods that are less damaging to ocean floors such as longlining, hook-and-line fishing and trap fishing rather than bottom trawling or dragging. One example is America's artisanal albacore fishery on the Pacific coast, where the fish are caught with pole and line using a centuries-old traditional Portuguese method.

GENERAL RECOMMENDATIONS

There is a world of resources available to all consumers about what to eat, when, and why. We have included as many in this book as space allows.

A FISHMONGER'S TAXONOMY

IMPORTANT FISH FAMILIES

Some international sources cite more than 31,000 unique fish species and almost 280,000 common names. The following families are some of the most important food fish families and their members.

CARANGIDAE (JACK FAMILY): HAMACHI, AMBERJACK, POMPANO, PALOMETA
Mostly found in marine water in the Atlantic, Indian, and Pacific oceans, this is one of the most important families of tropical sea fish for commercial and recreational fishing.

CICHLIDAE (TILAPIA FAMILY): GALILEE ST. PETER'S FISH, NILE TILAPIA, MOZAMBIQUE TILAPIA
The third most important farmed fish worldwide after carp and salmon with about 100 species in the family. Farmed tilapia are sold live from tanks at some fish markets or in restaurants. Worldwide tilapia production is predicted to reach 4 million tonnes (or metric tons, each 1000 kg).

CLUPEIDAE (HERRING FAMILY): HERRING, SARDINE, SHAD, PILCHARD, LAKE HERRING, MENHADEN (USED FOR PROCESSING)
One of the most important families of commercial fish, these oil-rich fish have global distribution and are found mostly in marine waters; some are freshwater and anadromous (that is, they live partly in fresh water and partly in salt water).

ENGRAULIDAE (ANCHOVY FAMILY): MEDITERRANEAN ANCHOVY, PACIFIC ANCHOVY
This commercially important family of small schooling fish is found in the Atlantic, Indian, and Pacific oceans, mostly in shallow coastal waters and estuaries in tropical and temperate regions. This is a very important preserved fish.

GADIDAE (COD FAMILY): PACIFIC COD, ATLANTIC COD, HADDOCK, WHITING, ALASKA POLLOCK
Found in the Arctic, Atlantic, and Pacific oceans, this cold-water family is second only to the Clupeidae (herrings) in volume of world catch. Atlantic and Eastern cod are on Seafood Watch's red list, but Pacific cod from Alaska is a best choice.

ICTALURIDAE (NORTH AMERICAN CATFISH FAMILY): CHANNEL CATFISH, BLUE CATFISH
Catfish are an important aqua-farmed fish, especially in the United States, where it accounts for over 40 percent of farmed fish sales.

LUTJANIDAE (SNAPPER FAMILY): RED, LANE, YELLOWTAIL, VERMILION, HAWAIIAN OPAKAPAKA AND UKU, JOBFISH
Not all snappers are members of this family of fish found in tropical and subtropical waters of the Atlantic, Indian, and Pacific oceans. They are of high value for food, though sometimes a cause of ciguatera poisoning.

MERLUCCIIDAE (HAKE FAMILY): HAKE, HOKI, GRENADIER
These voracious predators inhabit the continental shelf and upper slope with three species that live in large schools on the continental shelf in Sub Antarctic waters. They are found in the Atlantic and eastern Pacific oceans, and in the waters of Tasmania and New Zealand.

MORONIDAE (SEA BASS FAMILY): EUROPEAN SEA BASS, STRIPED BASS, FRESHWATER WHITE BASS
Members of this family, including the prized European sea bass (*loup de mer* in French, *branzino* in Italian), are found in fresh, brackish, and marine waters in North American Atlantic and Gulf of Mexico waters, Europe, and North Africa.

PERCIDAE (PERCH FAMILY): LAKE PERCH, RIVER PERCH
These fresh- and brackish-water fish are found in the northern hemisphere.

PLEURONECTIDAE (FLOUNDER FAMILY): DOVER SOLE, FLOUNDER, DAB, HALIBUT, PLAICE, TURBOT, PETRALE SOLE
These bottom-fish swim in the Arctic, Atlantic, Indian, and Pacific oceans. Almost all members of this family are food fish.

SALMONIDAE (SALMON FAMILY): SALMON, TROUT, ARCTIC CHAR, LAKE WHITEFISH
These fish live in the northern hemisphere but have been introduced in cold waters worldwide for sport fishing and aquaculture. Many are anadromous, living in both fresh and salt waters.

A FISH BY ANY OTHER NAME

Names sell: The slow-growing fish that used to be known as New Zealand slimehead was basically wiped out once it was renamed by marketers as the colorful orange roughy. Patagonian toothfish sells infinitely better as Chilean sea bass, again to the point of it being endangered in Chilean waters.

At market, the same fish may be sold under many different and confusing names, due to regional differences and the fact that a better name means faster sales and higher prices. Pacific Dover sole is neither from Dover nor is it a true sole; rather, it is a kind of flounder. Dover sole, found only on the European side of the Atlantic, is highly valued, so appropriating its name helps this lesser cousin sell better. Seafood preferences are very regional.

SCOMBRIDAE (TUNA FAMILY): BONITO, TUNA, MACKEREL, WAHOO, KINGFISH

Members of this family are among the most important of commercial and sport fish. Spanish mackerels, bonitos, and tunas feed on other fish, crustaceans, and squid.

SEBASTIDAE (PACIFIC ROCKFISH FAMILY): CHILIPEPPER ROCKFISH, VERMILION ROCKFISH, CANARY ROCKFISH, ROSE FISH, OR OCEAN PERCH

Found in the Atlantic, Indian, and Pacific oceans, about 110 species in this family live mainly in the North Pacific.

SERRANIDAE (GROUPER FAMILY): RED GROUPER, BLACK GROUPER, BLACK SEA BASS

This family of fish living in tropical and temperate oceans includes 449 species, many of them prized for food.

SPARIDAE (SEA BREAM FAMILY): DENTEX, PORGY, SHEEPSHEAD, SCUP, GILT-HEAD BREAM

Found in tropical and temperate waters of the Atlantic, Indian, and Pacific oceans. In the kitchen, the most celebrated are dentex and gilt-head bream.

XIPHIIDAE (THE SWORDFISH FAMILY): SWORDFISH

This family has a single member, swordfish, which swim in tropical and subtropical waters worldwide and are of high commercial value.

MAJOR SEAFOOD FAMILIES

Around the world, people enjoy eating "fruits of the sea" as diverse as Florida Stone crabs and Spanish gooseneck barnacles, Australian spiny lobsters and English periwinkles. Here, I have organized the non-fish sea creatures into mollusks, crustaceans, cephalopods, and echinoderms.

SINGLE-VALVED MOLLUSKS: ABALONE, CONCH, AND PERIWINKLES

Mollusks get their name from a Latin word, *mollis*, meaning "soft," because they all have soft meat, though some have very hard outer shells. Members of this uni-shelled family are also known as gastropods.

BI-VALVED MOLLUSKS: MUSSELS, CLAMS, OYSTERS, AND SCALLOPS

Members of this family include the many types of oysters, clams, mussels, and scallops found worldwide.

CEPHALOPODS: OCTOPUS, SQUID AND CUTTLEFISH

Members of this family have a thin, clear "bone" inside their bodies instead of a hard shell.

CRUSTACEANS

These have symmetrical bodies covered with a hard outer shell that must be shed periodically in order for the animal inside to grow larger. This group includes many species in high demand such as shrimp, lobsters, and crabs, but also fresh or brackish-water crayfish, rare gooseneck barnacles, langoustines or Dublin bay prawns, and Chilean langostino.

ECHINODERMS

Sea cucumbers and sea urchins are echinoderms, which get their name from two Greek words meaning "hedgehog skin."

CHOOSING FRESH WHOLE FISH

Skin and Coating: The fish should look as close to alive as possible with shiny, moist skin. Fish secrete a protective slime coat that covers scales and skin and acts as protective armor. Catfish and trout have especially thick coatings. The coating should be transparent.

Flesh: The fish should be firm enough to stay relatively stiff when picked up. The flesh itself should be so firm and taut that when it's pressed, it springs back without leaving a depression. Red bruises on the flesh indicate that the fish was injured during capture.

Grain: The grain of the flesh should be dense without gaps between the layers. These gaps will be especially noticeable in larger fish such as salmon or bluefish. If the fish is in a plastic-wrapped container, make sure there is no liquid that has leaked into the package, a sign of age.

Aroma: The fish should smell briny and oceanlike or, for freshwater fish, like a clean pond with no muddy aroma.

Scales and Gills: The scales should adhere tightly. Lift up the gill cover and examine the gills. They should be cherry-red, not at all brownish, a sign of oxidation.

Eyes and Tail: With the exception of a few deep-water fish such as grouper, the eyes should be clear and protruding. (Grouper eyes are naturally cloudy, even when fresh.) The tail should be moist and flat, not dry or curled up.

CHOOSING FRESH FISH FILLETS

The freshest fillets will be the most translucent with a moist appearance. Any reddish to pink color should be just that, without the brownish tint that develops as the blood oxidizes. Top-quality fish will often be bled upon capture.

Opaque fish fillets may be old or may have been chemically treated, especially inexpensive flounder fillets and block-frozen fish destined for fish sticks.

Choose center-cut fillets for best appearance when cooking individual portions. Choose the often less expensive head or tail end cuts when cutting the flesh into smaller pieces (for kabobs) or when cooking and picking off the flesh, as for salad. Keep in mind that there will be more waste for these cuts, though they should also be lower in price.

Look for freshly cut fish steaks or fillets. Pass up the last pieces of a fish cut earlier in the day or even the day before. The smaller the cut of fish, the faster it will deteriorate.

STORING FISH

Above all, keep fish cold. In the kitchen, ideally surround it with crushed ice and place it in a perforated pan or colander with another pan underneath to catch the drips. (Cubed ice can bruise the delicate flesh.) Alternatively, place the fish in a plastic bag, then top it with "blue ice" used in a cooler chest or a disposable freezer gel-pack.

Store in the coldest part of the refrigerator: in a drawer, not on the door. Cooking it the same day you buy it is best; if the fish is fresh and you keep it cold, it should keep two days from time of purchase. The bigger the piece, the better it will keep, so it's best not to cut fish into individual steaks until ready to serve them.

Whole, cleaned, and gutted fish will keep better than fillets. Also, the blood-rich gills deteriorate quickly, so it's best to have them removed at the market or pull out the sharp-edged gills using your hands in protective gloves or a pair of pliers.

CHOOSING AND PREPARING FROZEN FISH AND SEAFOOD

Buy frozen fish in a market where the turnover is high. The freezer itself should be quite cold, clean, and with minimal frost.

Check that the product is somewhat shiny and has no white freezer-burn spots, which come from exposure of the flesh to drying freezer air.

The product should be rock-hard with no evidence of previous defrosting, such as ice crystals. The package should be well sealed, preferably in heavy plastic and at most, three months old.

Thaw frozen fish in the refrigerator overnight. If that is not possible, place the sealed package in a bowl of cold water, changing the water several times as it chills. (If the fish is not already in a sealed package, place in a closed plastic freezer bag.) Never use warm water and never ever use the microwave or you'll end up with dry, fibrous fish. The fish is ready when it is mostly, but not completely, thawed.

Cook the fish the same day it is ready, because defrosted fish (and seafood) will leak its juices and will deteriorate quickly.

COOKING FISH

Ideally, fish is ready when it's barely done in the middle, so it's still juicy.

Most white-fleshed fish are quite lean and are easily overcooked till they become dry. Oily white Chilean sea bass, escolar, and black cod (known as sablefish, especially when smoked) are exceptions.

Fish that have delicate, soft flesh, such as sea bass, flounder, and red snapper, are especially vulnerable to overcooking. They take well to moderate-temperature cooking such as baking in juicy sauce, and pan-frying (with a coating to help protect the flesh).

Most darker and red-fleshed (salmon) fish are high in the oils that help keep them moist in cooking. These fish take well to high-temperature cooking methods such as roasting, grilling, and broiling.

When sautéing, get the pan really hot so the fish browns well and cooks quickly. The fresher the fish, the less you need to cook it. The highest quality tuna is only seared on the outside, while salmon is often served medium-rare, like a steak.

To keep the inside rare while still getting a brown crust on the outside, super-chill the fish by placing it in the freezer for 30 minutes before cooking. Cook most fish until the flesh is barely opaque and the flesh is just barely flakeable.

STORING SEAFOOD

For live seafood, such as crabs, clams, oysters, mussels, and lobsters, storage temperatures should be higher, ideally about 40°F (4°C). The goal is to keep the product moist and alive. Any of these creatures should show an immediate reaction when poked. Surround the product with seaweed, sea grasses, or damp newspapers to insulate and protect them from too much cold, which will kill them.

Store non-live seafood such as shrimp; crabmeat; crab claws; and cooked lobsters, crabs, shrimp, shucked oysters, mussels, and scallops in a container buried in ice so they stay as cold as possible.

Shellfish eaten raw on the half shell, such as oyster and clams but sometimes mussels and scallops, must be alive until just before they're opened up. Keep them ice cold, work clean, and serve as soon as possible after shucking.

For dredged seafood such as clams, wild mussels, and sometimes crabs, scrub well to remove grit but only just before cooking, because washing shortens shelf life.

SEAFOOD SAFETY TIPS

Avoid cross-contamination by keeping raw seafood juices away from other foods and using a separate, washable cutting board.

If your immune system is compromised, avoid eating raw fish or seafood.

It is safer to eat raw oysters and clams harvested from colder northern waters where the vibrio bacteria (red tide) doesn't grow.

Never eat dead shellfish. Clams, mussels, oysters, and live scallops should have unbroken tightly closed shells. Lobsters, crayfish, and crabs should move their claws vigorously when poked.

Cook seafood to an internal temperature of 145°F (63°C), and cool cooked seafood as rapidly as possible in ice mixed with ice water.

Although they are quite rare, be sensitive to seafood allergies and avoid eating any seafood that causes you to have an allergic reaction.

KNOW YOUR TERMS AT THE FISHMONGER'S

Whole Round: A whole fish that has been gutted and scaled with, often, the fins trimmed. For most fish, allow three-quarters to one full pound (346 to 453 g) per serving.

Pan Dressed Fish: A fish that has been gutted and scaled with head, tail, and fins removed for pan frying. Allow one half to three-quarters of a pound (227 to 340 g) per serving.

Fish Steak: These grill- or pan-ready cross-wise slices are cut from larger fish, such as salmon, halibut, or cod. Allow one-third to one-half pound (150 to 227 g) per serving.

Fish Fillet: Ready-to-cook portions of fish cut lengthwise from the fish with the backbone removed. The pin bones may be removed on request. Skin-on fillets allow the buyer to identify the fish and will keep better and shrink less in cooking.

Fish Skin: Because of the fat it contains, the skin helps to keep the fish moist and with less shrinkage in cooking. Leave the skin on, cook, then remove if desired. Soft-fleshed fish, such as red snapper and bluefish, are not skinned, because they would fall apart. Fish with inedible skin, such as catfish and grenadier, are sold skinned. (Eel have inedible skin and are always sold live.)

Deep-Skinned Fish Fillets: Some fish, including tilapia and triggerfish, have had the fatty, strong-tasting layer that lies just below the skin removed.

Whole Fillets: Fillets that include the entire side of fish with only the backbone removed, including the belly and nape (the lower side of the fillet below the center line at the head end of the fish). Allow one-third to one-half pound (150 to 227 g) per serving.

J-Cut and V-Cut Fillets: J-cut fillets have the backbone and small pin bones removed along with the nape. The thin belly meat just behind the nape may also be removed. V-Cut fillets have the backbone and small pin bones removed along with a thin triangular central section of darker meat at the head end of the fish. Allow one-third to one-half pound (150 to 227 g) per serving.

Tail On or Off: The tail meat is thin and stringy and curls up in cooking, so it is less visually appealing. It can easily be overcooked. The tail may be completely removed or "cropped," trimmed to make a neatly squared-off end.

FISHING METHODS

Dredging: A dredge is a heavy metal rake that is dragged across the ocean floor, scraping up most everything in its path. Dredging is used mainly for shellfish, especially scallops and clams, but also for blue crabs, which burrow into the sand in cold weather. The negative effect of dredges on ocean floor habitats is of concern. New habitat-friendly gear is being developed. Quality is directly related to the amount of time the dredge is in action—longer times means more sand is churned up.

Gillnetting: Curtains of netting are suspended by a system of floats and weights either anchored to the sea floor or allowed to float at the surface. Because the netting is almost invisible to fish, they swim right in. Gillnets are often used to catch sardines, salmon, and cod, but can accidentally entangle and kill other animals, especially sea turtles and sharks.

Longlining: A central fishing line as much as 50 miles (80 km) long; this line is strung at evenly spaced intervals with smaller lines of baited hooks. The longline can be set near the surface to catch pelagic fish such as tuna and swordfish that live in the open sea, or laid on the sea floor to catch bottom fish such as cod and halibut. The lines can also inadvertently hook sea turtles, sharks and seabirds that are also attracted to the bait. Sinking longlines deeper and using special hooks helps fishers reduce bycatch.

Purse Seining: One or two boats use a large wall of netting to encircle a school of pelagic (open-sea) fish such as mackerel, herring, and sardines, or species that gather to spawn, such as squid. Fishermen then pull closed the bottom of the net, which is shaped like a drawstring purse, herding the fish into the center. Depending on the purse seine used, some can catch other animals, such as the dolphins that can be caught in yellowtail tuna fishing. Quality is related to volume: The more fish are caught, the lower the quality tends to be.

Trawling and Dredging: Trawls and dredges are nets towed at various depths to catch fish or shellfish. Trawl nets are either dragged along the sea floor or midway between the floor and the surface. Trawlers catch fish such as pollock, cod, flounder, and shrimp. Bottom trawling can result in high levels of bycatch. Dredging involves dragging a heavy frame with an attached mesh bag along the sea floor to catch animals living on or in the mud or sand; catches include scallops, clams, and oysters. Dredging can damage the sea floor by scraping the bottom and also often results in significant bycatch.

Traps and Pots: Traps and pots are submerged wire or wood cages that attract fish with bait and hold them alive until fishermen return to haul in the catch. Traps and pots are usually laid on the ocean floor and connected by ropes to buoys on the surface; they are used to catch lobsters, crabs, and shrimp. They generally have lower unintended catch and less sea floor impact than does mobile gear such as trawls.

Harpooning: Harpooning is a traditional method for catching large fish and is still used today on a very small scale by skilled fishermen. When a harpooner spots a fish, he thrusts or shoots a long aluminum or wooden harpoon into the animal and hauls it aboard. Harpooners catch large, pelagic predators such as bluefin tuna and swordfish. Harpooning is an environmentally responsible fishing method. Bycatch of unwanted marine life is not a concern because harpoon fishermen visually identify the species and size of the targeted fish before killing it.

Trawl: This sock-shaped net has a wide mouth tapering to a small, pointed end that is towed behind a boat, scooping up everything in its path. Trawls are either dragged along the sea floor or midway between the floor and the surface. Trawls are used to harvest ground fish such as cod, flounder, and shrimp. The negatives here are that the product can be damaged by the weight of the catch and there can be a great deal of bycatch.

Trolling: For trolling, hook-and-lines are slowly dragged behind or alongside the fishing vessel with different lures and baits used to "troll" for different fish at different depths. This method is used to catch fish such as salmon, mahimahi, and albacore tuna that will follow a moving lure or bait. Trolling is environmentally responsible because the fish are caught on individual lines. Unwanted catch can be quickly unhooked and returned to the water because the lines are reeled in soon after a fish takes the bait. The fish will be of high quality (and usually fetch higher prices) because one fish at a time is hooked, cleaned, bled, and then iced or frozen onboard.

Polling: In polling, large numbers of surface-swimming fish such as yellowfin tuna are attracted to bait thrown into the water. The fish are caught on hooks attached to a pole and pulled on board, so bycatch is low to none.

PROFESSIONAL FISHMONGERS AND CUTTERS RELY ON A FEW GOOD TOOLS—NOT NECESSARILY EXPENSIVE BUT STURDY AND RELIABLE. MANY SPECIALTY SUPPLIERS SELL DIFFERENT VERSIONS OF THE SAME BASIC TOOLS. NO MATTER WHAT KNIFE YOU USE, THE MOST IMPORTANT THING IS TO KEEP YOUR TOOLS CLEAN AND SHARP.

A FEW GOOD TOOLS

1 SMALL STAINLESS STEEL FISH PLIERS are designed to pull out the pin bones contained in most fish. Many expert cutters prefer standard needlenose pliers from the hardware store.

2 There are many types of FISH SCALERS, from the simplest toothed tool to electric scalers. This heavy-duty scaler consists of four rings of toothed stainless steel and works well for larger fish. You can also use a chef's knife and scrape against the direction of the scales— a duller knife works best.

3 This STAINLESS STEEL FISH FILLETING KNIFE has a sealed plastic handle for sanitation. Some fish filleting knives are slightly flexible, making it easier to follow the shape of the fillet. This knife is not flexible but is strong enough for cutting larger fish. (See the longer version, the skinning knife, in "Skinning and Filleting Skate Wings.")

4 SHEARS are indispensable for cutting fish and preparing seafood. The large-handled shears shown here are preferred by many professional cutters, but other types will work as long as they are sharp and reasonably heavy.

5 A CLAM KNIFE has a rounded tip to avoid cutting into the clam meat and usually a sharpened blade on the inside for scraping the meat from the shell. They may have a sealed plastic handle and should be dishwasher safe. A thick comfortable non-slip handle helps prevent injury—of special concern because if the knife slips, it can puncture the skin deeply with live bacteria that can easily get infected. (The clam knife is also used to clean abalone in "Cleaning Live Abalone.")

6 The OYSTER KNIFE comes in many shapes and sizes, some short and squat, others long and narrow. For the professional shucker, the knife must be durable enough to last through shucking thousands of oysters yet light enough to be able to work quickly without tiring. This oyster knife is known as a Boston or Cape Cod shucker and is a venerable design. It has a narrow, thin, unsharpened triangular-shaped blade and a blunt end. Some oyster knives have a curved tip; others have a guard separating the blade from the handle. As with the clam knife, a non-slip handle helps prevent injury and potential infection.

7 To prevent injury, we recommend wearing a **PROTECTIVE GLOVE** on your non-shucking hand for better grip when shucking oysters, clams, and other bivalves. The glove shown here is made from polyester woven with stainless steel. Some gloves are made entirely from steel mesh; others from Kevlar (bullet-proof material).

8 This special **GUTTING KNIFE** is designed for gutting fish and for removing roe from fish such as shad. It has a rounded tip to prevent cutting into the viscera with a sharp, curved cutting edge. A fully sealed plastic handle is important for cleanliness.

MATERIALS NEEDED:

Fish scaler

Clean work surface

Newspaper (for cleanup)

Sink or large bowl of cold water (for rinsing)

Heavy kitchen shears

Large spoon

Kitchen towel or glove

Plastic film or butcher's paper (for wrapping)

1 Remove the fish from its container, drain, and pat it dry with paper towels. Lay fish on a clean work surface.

SCALING, GUTTING, AND TRIMMING LARGE ROUND FISH

The hybrid striped bass is a farm-raised fish that combines the distinctive appearance and good eating qualities of the wild striped bass with the hardier, faster-growing white bass, *Morone americana*. The fish weigh 1 to 2 pounds (450 to 900 g) and have mild, moderately firm flesh. Hybrid striped bass are farmed in ponds and tanks that limit water pollution and spread of disease. They are a good (if unexciting) fish to serve for two and are widely available throughout the year in many markets.

The magnificent silver and black striped bass, *M. saxatilis*, is native to North America, related to the European bass, or *branzino* (see "Filleting Round Fish, Butterfly Style"), and gets its name from the seven or eight prominent dark horizontal stripes along its silvery sides. Legendary among sport fishermen for their fighting ability, striped bass, or rockfish, are a favorite saltwater game fish for their striking appearance, fighting ability, and succulent, firm, white, flesh.

Most round fish, including red and other snappers, black sea bass, croaker, drum, grouper, walleye, whitefish, salmon, trout, Pacific rockfish, and pollock, may be scaled and gutted using this technique.

Start by setting up a table outdoors or cover a work surface and the floor with newspaper to make cleanup easier. A high table will be more comfortable, especially if it can be rinsed off easily with a garden hose or a bucket of water.

3 Grasp the fish just behind the head in your nonwriting hand. Using heavy kitchen shears, snip off the dorsal fins, cutting from the tail end toward the head.

2 Place fish with its belly toward you and its head toward your nonwriting hand. Grasp the head in your nonwriting hand using a cloth or glove for better grip. With a dull knife or fish scaler, scrape from the tail toward the head, against the direction of the scales. Keep your strokes short and quick. Turn the fish over and repeat. Work carefully around the fins as they are sharp enough to puncture your skin. Make sure to remove all scales from around the pectoral and dorsal fins, and up to the throat, or the edge of the fish's gills. Rinse the fish well under cold water. Clean the table.

4 Snip off about 1 inch (2.5 cm) from the tail fin. Snip off the pectoral fins just behind the gills, cutting from the belly toward the backbone. Snip off the remaining fins—the pelvic fins on the belly and the anal fin on the belly.

5 Using heavy kitchen shears, cut open the front end of the belly, starting just below the gills.

6 Continue cutting past the anal opening. Spread open the abdomen with your fingers and gently pull out the viscera, severing them at the throat and tail ends. (Any roe is considered a delicacy and should be removed in one piece. See "Shad: Extracting Roe, Filleting, and Boning"). Use a large spoon to scrape out the cavity.

7 Pull open the gill covers to expose the rosy-red gills. Push out the gills gripping them in a towel or glove as they are quite sharp. Use shears to cut away the gills, which are attached at either end on both sides of the head.

8 Open up the fish from the belly side, exposing the dark red kidneys that run just above and on either side of the backbone. Grasping the gill end of the fish in your nonwriting hand, use the tip of a knife or shears to slice open the kidneys.

9 With your knife, shears, and/or your fingers, scrape away all the dark red tissue. Rinse out the cavity under running cold water and pat dry inside and out. Either wrap the fish in plastic film and refrigerate on a tray to catch drips for use later or continue with your recipe. Your scaled and gutted fish is ready.

MATERIALS NEEDED

Paper towels

Clean cutting board

Fish filleting knife
(see "A Few Good Tools")

Sink or large bowl of cold water
(for rinsing)

Container to store fish fillets

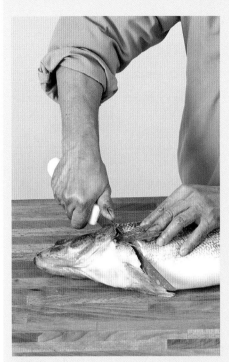

1 Lift up the gill fin and make a deep diagonal cut behind the fin, angling the knife toward the front of the fish to reach the flesh that extends under the bony plate of the skull. Cut from the head toward the belly in a single, smooth motion to avoid tearing the delicate flesh.

FILLETING A LARGE ROUND FRESHWATER FISH

For this technique, we use walleye (also known as walleye pike or pike perch), *Sander vitreum*, a freshwater fish. Ichthyologists (fish scientists) believe the ancestors of walleyes originated in Europe and moved across the Bering Sea land bridge to North America. Walleye is closely related to the European pike perch and is the largest member of the perch family. Like other perch, it has large, spiny dorsal fins. Its long, tapering body has olive-brown and golden-yellow markings on a silvery background—the fish are called *doré* in French for their golden color. Even when fresh, walleyes have cloudy eyes adapted to the dim light in which they forage. Their name comes from their resemblance to a blinded, or "walleyed," animal.

In the nineteenth century, walleye brought such a high price and was so much in demand that it became almost extinct. The rare European sander (*S. lucioperca*), also known as pike perch, is almost identical to walleye and is also found in Russia. As "yellow pike," walleye is commonly ground with whitefish and carp for Jewish *gefilte* fish (poached fish dumplings). Walleye may reach 25 pounds (11.4 kg), but 2 to 3 pounds (900 to 1350 g) is average. Their meat is succulent, ivory-white, and firm with few bones, and fine flake. Its yield is about 45 percent.

To begin, rinse the pike under cold water and pat dry. Place the fish on a clean cutting board with its top end facing your body and with the head end facing your writing hand. It is not necessary to gut the fish if you're filleting it.

2 Make three cuts on each side. For the first cut, bring the tip of the knife around to the back of the fish and slice just above the backbone toward the tail, cutting the flesh about one-third of the way through its width, following the bones by "feeling them" with the knife. Rest your nonwriting hand on the fish to steady it.

3 For the second cut, switch directions, working from the tail end toward the head and severing the fillet at the head end. Cut away the fillet about two-thirds of the way through its width while grasping the free end in your nonwriting hand.

4 Switch directions again, cutting from the head toward the tail and cut away the fillet completely over the belly flap either through or over the belly bones. Cut any remaining attached sinew or skin and remove the first fillet. Trim off the raggedy edges and the thinnest part of the belly.

6 Insert the knife into the fish just above the backbone at the tail end then cut the flesh about one-third of the way through its width while grasping the free end in your nonwriting hand.

7 Continue cutting, repeating steps 3 and 4 on the other side of the head, this time working from the head to the tail, then from the tail to the head.

5 The first fillet has been removed. Now you're ready to cut away the second fillet. Switch the direction of the pike so its head faces toward your nonwriting hand. Repeat step 1 on the other side of the head.

8 Trim the fillets into fairly regular shapes, cutting away the belly bones while holding the knife at a slight angle to the bones. Pictured: walleye pike bones with two fillets.

TIP

Fish are divided into two basic categories for processing: flatfish (such as flounder, turbot, sole, and halibut) and round fish (such as striped bass, cod, sable, and snappers), although many fish call for special filleting techniques including monkfish, cobia wahoo, mahimahi, John Dory, skate (see "Skinning and Filleting Skate Wings"), eel (see "Eel: Skinning and Preparing"), tuna (see "Cutting Tuna Loins"), swordfish, and pompano.

A CONSUMMATE FISHMONGER WHO KNOWS HIS CUSTOMERS ALMOST AS WELL AS HE KNOWS HIS FISH, JAY SILVER WORKS IN TANDEM WITH FRANK TORNETTA, WHO IS EQUALLY KNOWLEDGEABLE. BETWEEN SILVER'S JEWISH BACKGROUND AND TORNETTA'S ITALIAN BACKGROUND, THEY COVER THE WATERFRONT OF THEIR CUSTOMER BASE.

JAY SILVER:
RETAIL FISHMONGER FOR EIGHTEEN YEARS

Fishmongers Jay Silver and Frank Tornetta at their retail fish counter

They know who will be looking for what and when: carp, whitefish, and pike for gefilte fish at Passover and at Rosh Hashanah, and eels and bacala (salt-cod) at Christmas for the Feast of the Seven Fishes (La Vigilia) on Christmas Eve.

Silver didn't grow up in the fish business, although it was a typically Jewish business for generations. However, he is the son of a kosher butcher so, he says, food is "in my blood." Silver moved to the California Bay Area after high school and worked in numerous restaurants as a cook, which was his introduction to different kinds of fish and ways to use them. He later worked at Whole Foods in Berkeley, California, as a meat and seafood team member, which was his first taste of retail. He moved back East and began working at George's Dreshertown Shop n Bag in Philadelphia as the seafood department manager in 1991. Silver also teaches courses about seafood.

At this smallish though busy and extremely well-stocked market, the two fishmongers hold court every day for happy fish buyers.

We have a pretty good idea of what our customers want. The first thing they ask us is, "What's fresh today?"

WHY DO CUSTOMERS CHOOSE YOUR STORE?

Basically, we make it easy for them. We peel their shrimp, we cook the shrimp, we skin their fish, we walk them through our products. The two of us [Jay Silver and Frank Tornetta run the department] eat fish every day. Frank takes fish to his father; I take fish every day to my father and his girlfriend. We stand behind the counter here every day. It's George's name on the banner [George's Dreshertown Shop n Bag], but the customer doesn't know George; they know us. If something goes wrong, they're going to yell at us. Frank and I have each been working here for eighteen years so we have a pretty good idea of what our customers want. The first thing they ask us is, "What's fresh today?"

WHAT KIND OF SHELLFISH DO YOU SELL?

Our shrimp have no preservatives. They're just packed in saltwater—we make sure of that. Our Ocean Garden brand white Pacific shrimp from Mexico are top quality and we only carry untreated scallops. One day, a woman told me that she can buy scallops [elsewhere] at a much lower price. I answered, "Those scallops are treated [with TSP, trisodium phosphate) and have a totally different flavor." She said, "No, a scallop is a scallop is a scallop!" So, I gave her two of our natural scallops and asked her to let me know how it cooks up. She returned and admitted, "There really is a difference."

HOW ABOUT FARMED FISH— WHAT DO YOU SELL?

We carry conventional and organic Black Pearl salmon, which comes from the Shetland Islands and northern Scotland. As far as tilapia, if it's not fresh, we don't carry it. We did a taste test because tilapia can be dusty-tasting and decided on a sustainably raised brand from Costa Rica whose product contains no additives, preservatives, or growth enhancers.

HOW DIVERSE IS YOUR CLIENTELE?

We have a pretty big Jewish clientele who are very vocal about finding kosher fish [with fins and scales]. I don't make gefilte fish from scratch here, but I do grind fish for our customers. I'll grind carp, I'll grind whitefish. I'll clean it out, I'll chop the heads, I'll clean all the bones out. I take the eyes out, I scale it, I do all of that. So you have all the bones [to make the jellied stock], that I put it in a little separate bag. The Italians come at Christmas—the same people every year. We get the whiting, we get in the octopus, we do the seven fishes [that many Italians serve on Christmas Eve]. We get in the anchovies, sardines, calamari. We sold over 100 pounds (45.4 kg) of squid last Christmas. We even bring in eels, but not live. We have Asian customers and also some island people who might want the head of a fish.

WHAT DO YOU DO WITH YOUR SCRAPS?

I make fish stock with cod bones, bay leaf, and a little lemon. I put it in pint containers and freeze it. (Cod makes a very rich, full-bodied stock.) I'll also make shrimp stock. I make fresh salmon burgers from fresh salmon mixed with honey mustard, tarragon, and lemon pepper.

IS SUSTAINABILITY AN ISSUE FOR YOUR CUSTOMERS?

Some people will say, "I don't buy fish from farms" or "I don't want to buy this." A lady the other day said, "I won't buy Canada fish because they club their seals." We do carry some items that are Marine Stewardship Council–certified, but sustainability is not an important issue for our customers so far.

WHAT ARE PEOPLE EATING NOW?

Skate wings, believe it or not. We've been selling a lot of them. People aren't eating the same thing every week. We'll have skate one week, then the customers will take a couple of weeks off. We're selling a different shell oyster every week. We'll order in whole fish like branzino, pompano, and fresh sardines, which are a big thing now. We also try to keep everything at a reasonable price.

HOW DOES YOUR MARKET COMPARE TO THE COMPETITION?

We don't charge to shuck, we don't charge to cook or peel shrimp, we don't charge for steaming lobsters, we don't charge to fillet, scale, skin, or anything else the customer wants. At many markets, they don't have a deli guy, let alone a fish guy. We have only 12 feet (3.7 m) [of counter space] here but we move a lot of seafood, which forces us to keep everything fresh. If a customer says they won't like something, I'll cut up a small piece and send it home with them. Then maybe they'll buy more later and instead of just buying tilapia, they'll buy other things. Anything we can do for a sale, anything new to try, we're always going to do that.

TIP

Food scientist Harold McGee tells us in *On Food and Cooking* (Scribner 2004) that fish in the herring, salmon, and related families have these pin bones to "help stiffen some of the connective-tissue sheets and direct the muscular forces among them." Other members of the salmon family include steelhead, trout, whitefish, and Arctic char. Basically, the pin bones allow the fish to swim faster.

1 Use tweezers, special fish pliers, or needlenose pliers to remove the small pin bones, one for each muscle layer.

MATERIALS NEEDED

Paper towels or damp kitchen towel

Tweezers, needlenose pliers, or fish pliers

Container for fish

REMOVING PIN BONES FROM ROUND FISH

Most round fish have pesky pin bones that need to be removed before cooking. Also known as intermuscular bones, the pin bones are "floating" bones that are not attached to the main skeleton. Some experts use ordinary needlenose pliers to remove the bones; I prefer my small stainless steel fish pliers.

The pin bones start at the head end where they are longest and stiffest, and run about one-third of the length of the fish, gradually shortening and thinning with one bone per layer of flesh. Hold the fillet from underneath or place the fillet on an inverted bowl: The pin bones will poke out making them easier to find. Grab on to the pin bone while applying even, flat pressure to the fillet with your other hand. Pull out the

pin bone with a firm even tug, wiping your tweezers or pliers on a paper towel or damp kitchen towel in between. Always pull in the direction that the bones grow and pull toward your body to prevent tearing the delicate flesh of the fish. Inspect on the cut side of the fillet at the head end to locate the thicker harder pin bones. See "Boning Fish Steak and Making Fish Roulade" for instructions on removing the pin bones from a fish steak. Alternatively, cut out the pin bones in a very narrow V-shaped slice.

Here we remove the pin bones from a salmon fillet and a walleye fillet.

Turn the fish fillet so that the head end is toward your writing hand and the backbone faces you.

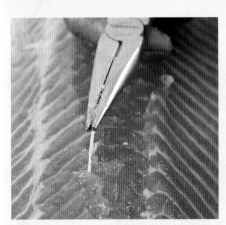

2 Continue pulling out the pin bones, which run about two-thirds of the way down the length of the fish. The bones will gradually get softer and thinner toward the rear of the fish.

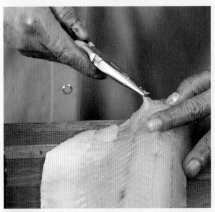

3 Here, we're removing the finer pin bones from a walleye pike fillet. Place the fillet with its head end toward you and its backbone side toward your nonwriting hand, using your nonwriting hand to steady the fish.

MATERIALS NEEDED:

Clean work surface

Kitchen shears

Sink or large bowl of cold water (for rinsing)

Kitchen towel or paper towels

CLEANING FISH THROUGH THE GILLS

This technique is used for neatly stuffing a whole fish, such as European seabass, trout, or salmon, before roasting, poaching, or grilling.

The European sea bass, *Dicentrarchus labrax*, is as sought after today as it was in Roman times. They are found in the ocean, saltwater lakes, and the lower reaches of rivers in Europe from the Mediterranean north as far as the UK, Iceland, and Norway. In Roman times, river fish were preferred; today saltwater bass are considered best. Both sea bass and the closely related spotted sea bass, *D. punctatus*, are known as *lavraki* in Greece, where aqua farms abound. Line-caught wild sea bass are tops in flavor and texture but are rare and expensive. Wild sea bass may reach 26 pounds (12 kg).

The fish are known as *spigola* in Southern Italy and *branzino* in Northern Italy—the name used on many menus where they often appear roasted or grilled whole in Mediterranean-style restaurants. Known in France as *bar* or *loup de mer*, meaning "sea wolf," they should not be confused with

the unrelated wolffish, *Anarhichas lupus*. Related to the striped bass (an alternative scientific name for them is *Morone labrax*), in Spain, the fish are called *lubina* or *róbalo*.

In Greece and Turkey, sea bass are grilled over natural charcoal and dressed with lemon juice, extra-virgin olive oil, and parsley. In France, they may be stuffed with an herb-scented savory, moist filling, perhaps including shrimp or scallops, then poached or roasted.

Farmed European sea bass are available year-round. These fish weigh $1\frac{1}{2}$ to 3 pounds (675 to 1350 g) and have a silvery skin much like striped bass without the stripes. This handsome and voracious pointy-nosed fish makes for excellent eating with firm, white, delicate flesh and no small bones. They hold their shape well when cooked—another reason they're popular in restaurants.

Here, we remove the viscera from a farmed branzino through the gills, cutting open the belly minimally.

1 Turn the fish belly up with its tail facing your nonwriting hand. Grasp underneath the middle of its body. Using shears, cut across the isthmus, or the "throat" of the fish, severing it.

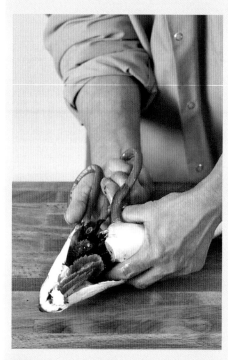

4 Using sharp kitchen shears, sever both sets of gills on either side of the head. Gills are sharp and you may want to wrap them in a towel or use a glove to protect your hand.

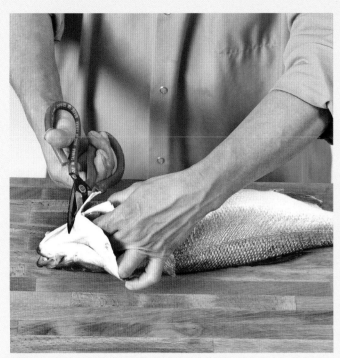

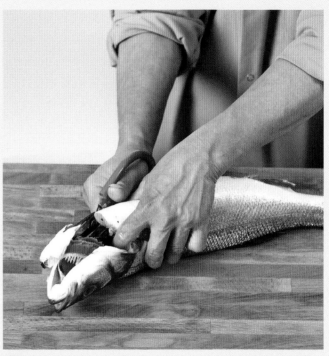

2 Grasping the free end of the backbone with your nonwriting hand, cut away the flesh all around the gill section.

3 Now you have a medium-large opening at the head end of the fish with the head disconnected on the belly side from its body. Using your nonwriting hand, and with the fish's belly facing up, pull back the body end of the fish to expose the gills.

5 Some of the viscera will come out attached to the gills. Cut away the viscera using shears.

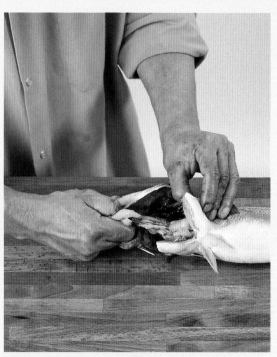

6 Make a cut about 2 inches (5 cm) long at the center line of the belly end toward the tail to be able to reach the remaining viscera.

7 Grasp the remaining viscera firmly and pull them out and away from the fish, cutting or pulling them completely free. Rinse the fish inside and out and pat dry.

8 The fish has now been completely gutted and is ready to stuff and cook.

CESARE CASELLA ALWAYS SPORTS A NOSEGAY OF FRESH GREEN HERBS PEEKING FROM HIS CHEF'S COAT POCKET. CASELLA'S PARENTS RAISED HIM AMONG THE POTS AND PANS IN THE KITCHEN OF VIPORE, THE SMALL TRATTORIA THEY OWNED NEAR LUCCA, ITALY, NOT FAR FROM THE TUSCAN COAST OF THE MEDITERRANEAN.

CESARE CASELLA:
PROPRIETOR OF SALUMERIA ROSI, NEW YORK CITY, AND DEAN OF THE ITALIAN CULINARY ACADEMY

Casella opened several successful restaurants in New York, serving his earthy, authentic, though rule-bending Tuscan cuisine with plenty of fresh seafood. His latest venture is Salumeria Rosi, serving cured meats and small plates. Chef Casella is dean of the Italian Culinary Academy and author of *Diary of a Tuscan Chef* (Doubleday, 1998), *Italian Cooking for Dummies* (IDG, 1998), and *True Tuscan* (Harper Collins, 2005).

HOW IS SEAFOOD OBTAINED FOR RESTAURANTS IN TUSCANY— DIRECT FROM FISHERMEN, DELIVERED TO YOUR DOOR, FROM A MARKET, AND SO ON?
[In Lucca, Tuscany], you eat the fish caught in the morning for lunch and in the afternoon the boats go back out and bring in fresh fish for dinner. Geographically, Italy is in an excellent situation to have fish so fresh that very little time passes between when it is caught and when it is prepared. Literally, sometimes less than an hour can pass between catching and cleaning fish in Italy. Our fish have what we call twenty-four hours of quality. Each hour after the fish is caught, you lose a bit of that quality. So, many Italian chefs have a problem cooking seafood outside of Italy because in other places, the seafood is generally not as fresh.

WHAT ARE YOUR FAVORITE TUSCAN SEAFOOD SPECIES?
Blackfish (*Centrolophus niger*), which is a type of sea bass. I also like arselle (also known as telline or wedge clam, these clams live in the swash zone of sandy beaches and were gathered by dragging a large strainer through the sand in the shallows).

San Pietro (Zeus faber, Saint Peter's fish, or John Dory) from Holland and New Zealand, because Italy doesn't harvest enough to supply its own demand.

DO YOU LIKE CRUDO? DO YOU SERVE IT AT YOUR RESTAURANT?

Italians have eaten crudo, which simply means "raw" in Italian, for centuries—mostly in fishing towns where the quality is superb. The fish is dressed simply with excellent extra-virgin olive oil and lemon with perhaps a few capers. I love crudo! I love it most when the fish is extremely fresh. Although we don't serve crudo at Salumeria Rosi, we do serve dishes like our *acciughe marinate*, white anchovies marinated in extra-virgin olive oil and vinegar with radicchio Trevisano.

DO YOU HAVE ANY "TRUCS OF THE TRADE" FOR HOME COOKS, SUCH AS WHAT TO LOOK FOR WHEN CHOOSING SEAFOOD OR COOKING TIPS?

When you choose seafood, it needs to speak to you—it needs to be happy and bright! When you see the eyes and they look dead, if the fish is not flexible, it is not good. Do not buy it! Really good fish should be cooked less and can be cooked more simply.

ARE THERE ANY UNDERUTILIZED SPECIES YOU'D RECOMMEND?

Dover sole and branzino may be top choices; it is better to look in your local market for fish that may be less prestigious, but are fresher. Freshness is the key. The best-kept secrets of a fish market: whiting, fresh sardines, kingfish (usually amberjack), and porgy, which is closely related to European sea bream. Local mackerel are fish that are great to use if you know how to use them in the right way!

WHAT MAKES TUSCAN SEAFOOD UNIQUE COMPARED TO SEAFOOD IN OTHER REGIONS OF ITALY?

Every region in Italy has its own type of fish. Toscana (Tuscany) has almost as much fish and coastline as Sicily, Italy's main seafood region, and its seafood is marketed in Rome and Milano. Every region's seafood's flavor and consistency will be different because of the geography of each region. With a coastline of more than 8,000 kilometers, annual consumption of seafood in Italy is high—about 23 kg (50 pounds) per capita.

Blackfish, which is a deepwater fish, is in season in fall. The best time to eat gamberetti (shrimp) is September. We eat *triglia*, red mullet, in late spring. Other places have their seasonal specialties like Venice's *moleche*, which are soft-shell rock crabs.

HOW DO PEOPLE IN TUSCANY LIKE TO PREPARE SEAFOOD?

Grilled or steamed. Only! Or in *insalata di mare*, seafood salad made from freshly steamed shellfish. The combination of seafood and beans such as the Tuscan *insalata di fagioli con tonno* (shell bean and tuna salad) is really an inland phenomenon that originated in Sicily, because preserved fish was used, like the canned or bottled tuna in this salad. In Italy, restaurants don't list many fish on the menu because they don't know what will show up that day from the market. The fishermen go out in small boats and catch a variety of fish but because of various regulations, they are only allowed to keep certain species. The fishermen may go out for anchovies but that's not necessarily what they'll catch.

ARE THERE ANY SEAFOOD SPECIALTIES THAT ARE ONLY FOUND IN TUSCANY?

Every region has a specific dish that it is great at. For instance, for fish soup, we know that there is *cacciucco* in Livorno, *buridda* in Sardinia, *brodetto* in Ancona. There is much more variety in seafood coming from other countries. That is a positive change for Italians! Because of market demand, fish such as salmon from Norway and elsewhere, sea bass from Israel, and lobster from Maine are showing up regularly in our markets. We also import

----

Chef Cesare Casella brings the food of Tuscany to the United States.

MATERIALS NEEDED:

Clean cutting board

Fish filleting knife (preferably a fish filleting knife)

Sink or large bowl of cold water (for rinsing)

Kitchen towel or paper towels

1 Lift up the gill fin and make a deep diagonal cut behind the fin, angling the knife toward the front of the fish to reach the flesh that extends under the bony plate of the skull and cutting from the belly toward the backbone.

FILLETING ROUND FISH, BUTTERFLY STYLE

In this technique, we remove the head and fins of a fish (shown here, branzino), and fillet it, keeping the tail section intact and the skin on. This method works well if you're planning to stuff and bake, broil, or grill a smaller fish.

To begin, lay the fish on a clean cutting board with its backbone toward you and its head facing your writing hand. (The fish should be scaled but does not have to be gutted.)

2 With a filleting knife, cut from head to tail without cutting through the tail, sliding the knife alongside the bones, "feeling them" with the knife. Angle the knife toward the bones rather than toward the flesh. Cut through the belly bones but don't cut through the tail.

3 Switch directions and cut from the tail end toward the head, cutting about two-thirds through the body width. While grasping the free end in your nonwriting hand, cut over the backbone.

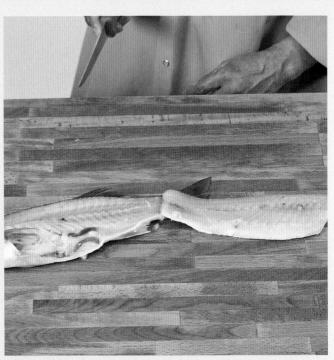

4 Switch directions again, cutting from the head toward the tail, and cut away the fillet completely through the belly bones. Cut away any attached sinew or skin and remove the first fillet. Cut the fillet away from the sides so that it is free at the head end but still attached at the tail.

6 Insert the tip of the knife just in front of the tail and cut toward the head about one-third of the way through the fillet. (You'll be leaving the two fillets attached at the tail end.)

7 Reverse directions and repeat, this time, cutting about two-thirds of the way through the fillet from head to tail.

5 To remove the second fillet, flip the fish so that its head end is facing your nonwriting hand. Lift up the gill fin and repeat step 1 on the other side of the head.

8 Insert the knife at the head end across the width of the fish while grasping the fillet. Cut to release the fillet completely from the sides leaving it attached at the tail end. End the cut 2 to 3 inches (5 to 7.5 cm) before the end of the tail.

9 Completed pocketbook filleted fish, ready for stuffing and baking.

TIP

To stuff a pocketbook filleted fish: Open up the top fillet and spread the stuffing on the bottom fillet. Cover with the top fillet, pushing the two fillets together to re-form the original shape of the fish.

TIP

To prepare a flatfish pocketbook style—a popular method in North and South Carolina and Florida—cut a slit down the dark center or lateral line of the fish above the spine, cutting through the skin and flesh until you reach the bone. Slide the knife under the flesh and above the rib bones at the head end on one side of the fish. Cut toward the tail, making an opening from the spine as far as the side fins without cutting through the skin. Repeat on the other side to make a second opening. Insert desired stuffing into the openings on either side of the spine, then push the two sides together to reform the original shape of the fish, and roast the fish whole.

MATERIALS NEEDED:

Clean cutting board

Filleting knife (preferably a fish filleting knife)

Kitchen shears

Sink or large bowl of cold water (for rinsing)

Kitchen towel or paper towels

1 Insert the tip of a filleting knife into the flesh just above the backbone at the head end and cut a slit all the way along one side of the backbone, from the head toward the tail.

BONING A ROUND FISH THROUGH THE BACK

Here we remove the backbone and rib cage of a fish (shown here, branzino). Use this method if you want to keep the head and tail intact and then stuff and bake a whole fish. It is a popular method in many French kitchens. A longer, narrower fish works best for this technique. Other fish suited to boning through the back include small bluefish, Arctic char, steelhead salmon, salmon, small wild striped bass, hybrid striped bass, whitefish, drum, trout, and sea trout.

A whole stuffed fish that has been boned as in this technique makes a dramatic and delicious centerpiece for a buffet dinner. Boning the fish makes it easy to cut into portion slices and a stuffed fish feeds more people. Use the bones that you have removed to make fish fumet as basis for a French-style reduction sauce.

To begin, place the scaled and gutted fish on its side on a clean cutting board with its backbone toward you and its head facing your writing hand.

4 Flip the fish over so that its backbone is toward you and the head is facing your nonwriting hand. Insert the knife above the backbone at the tail end and cut about one-third of the way through the fillet.

2 Switch directions and cut from the tail to the head, sliding the knife alongside the rib cage, cutting the flesh away from the backbone about one-third of the way through the body, sliding the knife alongside the bones, following the bones by "feeling them" with the knife. Leave the fillet attached at the tail end.

3 Reverse directions and cut from the head to the tail, cutting about two-thirds of the way through the fillet leaving it attached at the head and at the tail.

5 Reverse directions and cut from the head to the tail, cutting about two-thirds of the way through the fillet leaving it attached at the head, tail, and belly.

TECHNIQUE

REMOVING THE BACKBONE OF A FISH FROM THE STOMACH: Place a scaled and gutted fish on a clean work surface with its backbone facing away and its head end toward your writing hand. Enlarge the belly opening as far as possible toward the head and at the tail end, leaving the head and tail attached.

Lift up the side of the fish at the tail end and slide the knife along the upper side of the backbone and rib cage cutting it free from the flesh. Repeat on the other side of the backbone. Pull out the backbone then sever it at both ends. Fill the opening loosely with your preferred stuffing, then pat the fish back into shape before baking.

6 Fish with backbone exposed on both sides, ready to be removed.

7 Turn the fish so that its head faces your writing hand. Carefully lift out the backbone along with the attached rib cage and viscera. Using kitchen shears, cut through the backbone at the head end to sever it.

8 Grasp the backbone and viscera with your nonwriting hand and pull it out of the fish. Use the shears to cut away the remaining connective tissue attaching the backbone to the body of the fish, severing it completely but leaving the tail section whole.

9 Branzino with backbone, rib cage, and viscera removed, ready for stuffing. Thoroughly rinse the fish inside and out under running water and pat dry before stuffing as desired.

VELIA DE ANGELIS IS THE GASTRONOMIC CONSULTANT FOR *TASTE ITALIA MAGAZINE* AND IS A REGULAR GUEST CHEF ON ITALIAN TELEVISION'S *CHEF PER UN GIORNO*.

VELIA DE ANGELIS:
CHEF, COOKING TEACHER, AND CO-OWNER OF LA CHAMPAGNERIA, ORVIETO, ITALY

Personable and lively, de Angelis studied primary education then moved to the UK. There, she worked for Virgin Hotel Company (UK) in sales, marketing, and public relations while spending many hours in a secret restaurant to fulfill her passion for cooking. De Angelis returned to Italy with Virgin Company to open Palazzo Sasso, one of the most beautiful and luxurious hotels on the Amalfi Coast. She is co-proprietor with Gianluca Antoniella and chef of La Champagneria wine bar in her native Orvieto in Umbria and operates her school, Velia's Cooking Style, in the nearby town of Monterubiaglio. Starting in 2005, Velia has organized an annual cooking tour, teaching the best of *la cucina Italiana*.

DO YOU HAVE ANY "TRUCS OF THE TRADE" TO HELP US CHOOSE THE BEST FISH AND SHELLFISH?

With a little bit of common sense, anyone can recognize good seafood: a sparkling look on the outside for fish, mollusks, and crustaceans is the most important indicator of quality. Look for lively protruding eyes, rosy-red gills, and resilient-textured flesh. As far as processed seafood, check the label for the date of processing and its provenance. Remember that five days past the sell-by date, the product is still fresh.

I recommend buying crustaceans live. If the head has darkened or if one notices dark speckles on the exterior shell, the (lobsterette—*Nephrops norvegicus*) by the head, and it doesn't move or the body separates from the head, that tells you that it was harvested quite a few days before.

WHAT ARE YOUR FAVORITE KINDS OF FISH AND SHELLFISH?

I very much love *pesce azzurri*, the collective name for the whole range of red-fleshed fish that swim in the open waters of the Mediterranean gleaming with blue and silver skin like anchovies, sardines, and tuna. (Fish that swim close to the surface are known in Italy as *pesce bianchi*, or white-meat fish.) Pesce azzurri have fine eating qualities, cost less in the marketplace, and are best eaten fresh from the water.

REGIONAL ITALIAN SEAFOOD SPECIALTIES

BOTTARGA

Bottarga is made from dried eggs of tuna or *muggine* (or *cefalo*—gray mullet). To make bottarga, the filleted fish are covered with salt for several hours. Successively it is washed and then dried for some time in the fresh air and sun. Today, for protection against contamination, the fish is placed in a suitable oven where it rests for four to six hours at a temperature between 25°C and 30°C (77°F and 86°F). Afterward the fish is pressed and packed into glass.

MOSCIAME

Mosciame is made from the upper part of the tuna *ventresca*, or belly, from tuna fished during the traditional annual tuna hunt. This is a typical product of the coastal areas that is prepared on the spot, salted and dried in the fresh air. *Mosciame* was prepared by the fishermen themselves when they were out in the high seas. After having soaked the fish fillets in salt brine for several hours, they would hang the salted fish from the end of their boats to dry. When they returned to port, the fisherman and his family would eat the mosciame. Originally, the fish that they used to prepare mosciamo was dolphin [the mammal, not dolphinfish, which is mahimahi]. Today, because dolphin fishing is prohibited, tuna is substituted, or occasionally, swordfish (*pesce spada*) is used. *Mosciame* means "flaccid" or "withered", referring to the texture of the fish after it has been dried.

COLATURA DI ALICI

Colatura di alici is an amber-colored transparent liquid that is formed while soaking anchovies in a salt brine. It is a traditional food product of Campania made in the small fishing village of Cetara on the Amalfi Coast. There, the anchovies that are used for pressing are fished during the season that begins on March 25 (Feast of the Annunciation) until July 22 (the Feast of St. Mary Magdalene).

also love *la pezzogna* (*Pagellus bogaraveo*—blackspot seabream), which has tender, tasty flesh. Calamaretti (small squid), totanetti (small totano, *Illex coindetii*, broadtail shortfin squid harvested by artisanal fisheries throughout the Mediterranean), and shrimp are my favorites to prepare in seafood stew or to make the best-tasting dish of pasta. love raw octopus in salad combined with grains like farro (emmer wheat, *Triticum dicoccum*) or barley to create a diversity of preparations always rooted in tradition.

WHAT DIFFERENCES ARE THERE BETWEEN THE KINDS OF SEAFOOD YOU EAT IN ORVIETO AND WHAT YOU EAT IN AMALFI?

Orvieto, where I live and co-own La Champagneria, is a city built on *tufo* (a type of volcanic rock), not on the sea. To find seafood, one must travel to the coast. The choice is always based on the availability of product at the daily market. On the coast, one can find an ample choice in a region rich with seafood. It's beautiful to wake up in the morning and visit the port close to the docks where the fishermen pile up the live fish in front of your eyes. This happens only close to the sea. Let's not forget, however, that Italy's most important fish market is in the inland city of Milano.

HAVE YOU EVER EATEN DATTERI DI MARE? I UNDERSTAND THEY'RE OUTLAWED NOW, BUT I'D LIKE TO KNOW WHY THEY'RE SO SPECIAL.

Fishing for *datteri di mare* (sea date—*Lithophaga lithophaga*) is very invasive and destructive for the environment and the rocky coastlines that house these small mussels. Because of this, harvesting sea dates is forbidden. However, their flavor is distinctive, reflecting the place that they were harvested. I also want to mention the famous *patelle di mare* [a type of limpet] that live attached to rocks appearing at low tide. Compared to datteri di mare, patelle di mare have firmer, rather leathery flesh in which the essence of the sea is unmistakable.

1 Place the fish with its light side up, its backbone toward you, and its head facing your nonwriting hand. Grasp the head with your nonwriting hand right under the gills. Place the knife, preferably a fish filleting knife, at a 45-degree angle to the backbone just in back of the head.

FILLETING LARGE FLATFISH IN FOUR FILLETS

Here we fillet a large fluke into four fillets, a method that will yield the most fillet. This technique is best used to fillet large flatfish (over 3 pounds or 1.35 kg). This yields two smaller, lighter fillets cut from the underside and two larger, darker fillets cut from the topside. Because it's easier to remove the fillets from the first side of any fish, experts start filleting on the light side to make the more challenging task of removing the more tender, thinner light side fillets easier. (Because they actually swim on their sides, the backbone in all flatfish lies in the center of the body, not the top edge.)

Fluke, *Paralichthys dentatus*, has brownish skin with conspicuous black spots on top and an almost pure white bottom often with reddish areas where the delicate fish has been bruised. Called *hirame* in Japanese,

with their clear, delicate, pinkish white flesh, fluke are a sushi favorite. Fluke are the largest of the flounders, weighing up to 26 pounds (11.8 kg) and are the only commercially important left-eyed member of the large flounder family.

Another large flatfish suitable for filleting in four sections is Europe's prized turbot, *Scopthalmus maximus*, a left-eyed fish with nail-like knobs on its upper side and firm, full-bodied lean white meat. The turbot (not the same at Greenland turbot) is now farm-raised. Its yield is 50 percent, which is quite high.

The fluke shown here weighs about 3 pounds (1.35 kg).

Chef Velia de Angelis making one of her signature small plates

TIP

The snowy-white fin meat or fringe on a halibut and other flatfish is flavorful, dense, and full-bodied and is well worth keeping on for a large fish such as this one. It is known as *himo* in Japanese. The same name refers to the outer fringe of a clam.

2 Make a deep cut on the diagonal cutting toward the top of the head. Curve the knife around the top of the head. Always leave the head on because it provides a handle for grasping the fish.

3 Make a slit in front of the "fringe" (the wavy line of fins that surround the fish) from the head end toward the tail. Continue cutting until you reach the tail.

6 Insert the tip of the knife into the backbone 2 to 3 inches (5 to 7.5 cm) behind the head with the knife facing the head of the fish. Turn the knife so that it faces the tail of the fish and start cutting the second light fillet away from the body.

7 As the fillet is freed, grasp the end with your nonwriting hand.

4 Reverse directions. Grasp the end of the fillet with your nonwriting hand. Cut from the tail toward the head, about two-thirds of the way through the fillet toward the backbone. Repeat from the tail to the head, this time cutting all the way to the backbone (in the middle on a flatfish).

5 Lay the flat back down and now cut from the head toward the tail just on your side of the backbone to remove the first quarter-fillet. Lift off the freed fillet section and cut it away completely from the fish at the tail end.

8 Continue cutting, this time cutting all the way through the fillet at the edge of the body.

9 With the knife almost flat against the body, cut away the entire fillet working from head to tail. Cut through until you reach the tail to remove the second (larger) light fillet.

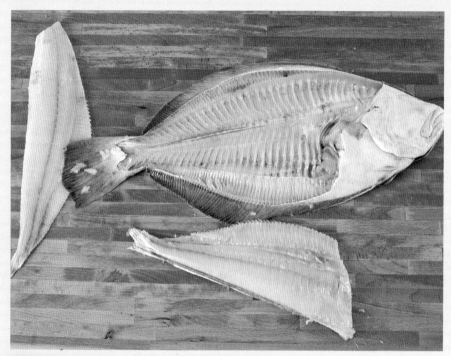

10 Fluke with bottom two fillets removed (and roe exposed).

11 Turn the fish over so that its dark side is up and its head is facing your nonwriting hand. Grasping its head in your nonwriting hand, make a diagonal cut in back of the head on the far side of the fish.

14 Continue cutting until you have released the fillet all along its outer edge, grasping its free end in your nonwriting hand.

12 Curve the knife around the head and make a second diagonal cut in back of the head at an angle to the first.

13 Insert the tip of the knife into the corner of the head where the two angles meet. Continuing the line of the first head cut, slice around the gut section of the fish (which you can see and feel with your hands) just in back of the head.

15 Lay the fillet back down and find the dark lateral line down the center of the fish and cut through it to the backbone, cutting from head to tail.

16 After making the cut, pull up the almost-free fillet with your nonwriting hand and cut the fillet completely free from the fish, cutting from head to tail, releasing the first (smaller) dark fillet.

17 Insert the tip of the knife into the flesh in back of the head above the backbone. Cut the fillet away on the backbone side, grasping the free end in your nonwriting hand.

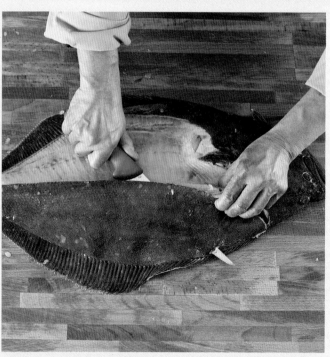

18 Lay the fillet flap back down and insert the knife all the way through the fillet at the head end. Cut until the second (larger) dark fillet has been completely freed from the fish.

19 Large fluke with four fillets removed. When cutting off the fillets, you may choose whether to leave the wavy edge fins on.

1 Grasp the head with your nonwriting hand. Make a small incision about 1 inch (2.5 cm) from the edge as a starter cut. Begin cutting the fillet free, keeping the knife almost flat.

FILLETING SMALL FLATFISH IN TWO FILLETS

Here we fillet a flatfish in two fillets using a smaller fluke, a left-eyed fish in the flounder family that weighs up to 8 pounds (3.6 kg). Flounder, found mostly in northern waters, are the most important family of flatfish. Their Latin name, *Pleuronectidae*, means "sideswimmer" because they swim on their sides. The fish start out round when young, and as they mature to become bottom-dwellers, one eye moves over to the same side of the head as the other eye and the fish turn on the side to swim.

Flounders spend their adult life in the ocean in summer and move into estuaries in cold weather. Atlantic flatfish include halibut (see "Cutting Fish Steaks from Halibut") as well as winter flounder, lemon sole, or common flounder (the last three are all the same species: *Pseudopleuronectes americanus*), summer flounder (fluke), and Greenland halibut or turbot, *Reinhardtius hippoglossoides*. Pacific flatfish include petrale sole, rex sole, Pacific sand dab, Pacific halibut, and California halibut. Some flounders are yellow on the underside of their tail.

To begin, lay a scaled and washed flatfish (fluke shown) with its light side up and its head facing your nonwriting hand. (Note that it is not necessary to gut the fish because you'll be filleting it.)

2 Continue cutting until you reach the tail.

3 Reverse directions with the knife and cut from the tail toward the head, this time cutting about 2 inches (5 cm) from the edge of the body until you reach the head.

4 Reverse directions again, now cutting from head to tail and grasping the free edge of the fillet with your nonwriting hand. Keeping the knife flat to the body, cut all the way through the fillet on both sides of the backbone, laying your knife flat against the backbone so that the fillet is completely free except where it is attached at the outer skin.

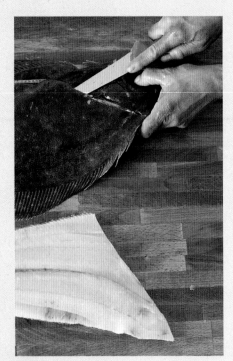

8 Cut around the head, then insert the tip of the knife just above the end of the back-bone just in back of the head. Lay the knife flat against the backbone while grasping the head with your nonwriting hand.

9 Keeping the knife flat, cut the belly side of the fillet away from the body following a curved line just ahead of the wavy fins.

10 Grasping the free end of the fillet in your nonwriting hand, repeat the cut, freeing the fillet up to the backbone.

5 Grasping the free end with your nonwriting hand, cut through the skin to release the entire light side fillet.

6 Light side (smaller) fillet with its wavy fin meat attached.

7 Turn the fish so that its dark side is up and its head is facing your nonwriting hand.

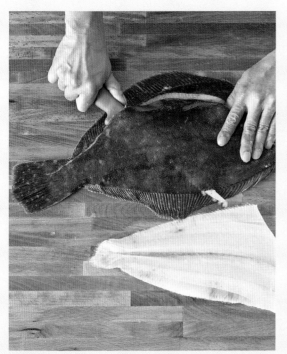

11 Insert the knife under the fillet and above the backbone diagonally across the width of the fish and cut through the outer edge of the skin just in front of the wavy fins, keeping the knife flat against the flesh. Cut through the skin to release the entire dark side fillet.

12 Fluke with thinner light fillet and thicker dark fillet ready for cooking.

MATERIALS NEEDED

Clean work surface or cutting board

Boning knife or filleting knife

Kitchen shears

Container for fish

FILLETING FLATFISH INSIDE OUT

In this method, adapted from glove-boning small birds, the entire rib cage and backbone is removed starting at the head, severing the ligaments connecting the bones at the head end, then turning the bird inside out. The same concept is applied here for "inside-out" fish, an excellent and uncommon technique to use when stuffing a whole (headless) fish. Other fish that can be successfully turned inside out include other flatfish such as petrale sole, plaice, small halibut, and yellowtail flounder.

Sometimes the inside-out fish are deep-fried with the flesh side out; sometimes they are turned right side out, stuffed and baked, broiled or grilled. Start with a scaled and gutted fish.

1 Place the fish (here a small fluke) with its dark side up and its head facing your nonwriting hand. Cut off the head, slicing on the diagonal from the head toward the belly.

4 Twist the knife around the edges of the rib cage and cut underneath the backbone to free the rib cage further.

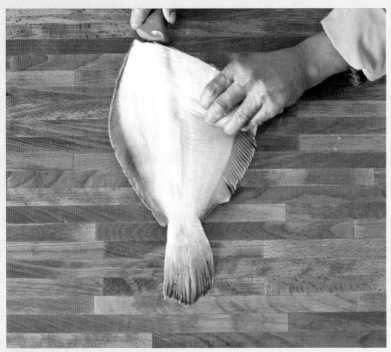

2 Turn the fish with its light side up. Insert the tip of the knife above the backbone and cut from the belly side toward the head without cutting through the skin on either side.

3 Turn the fish so that its dark side is up. Insert the knife under the backbone and cut from the head toward the belly without cutting through the skin on either side. This also frees the rib cage from the body.

5 Grasp the fish and curve it sharply at the head and tail end while pressing down in several places along the backbone to break it in two or three spots. This will make it easier to remove the rib cage.

6 Turn the fish with its light side up. Insert kitchen shears inside the fish along one side at the head end. Carefully cut the rib cage free from the body of the fish along both sides.

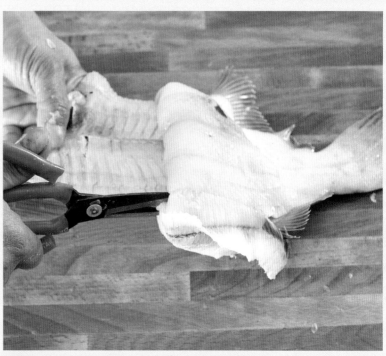

7 Fold the cut end of a fish about 1 inch (2.5 cm), as if folding back a shirt cuff. This exposes the rib cage. Continue folding the fish inside out, gradually so as not to break the fish.

8 Cut the rib cage away from the fish along both sides.

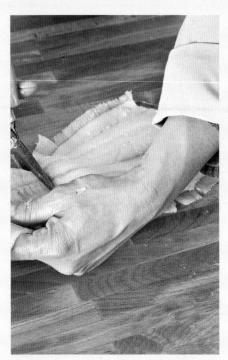

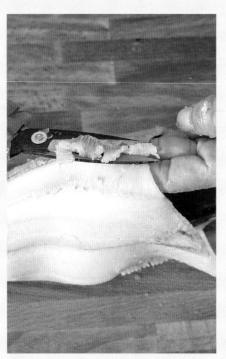

9 When the fish is completely folded and the rib cage completely freed on the sides, use the shears to snip off the rib cage at the tail end of the fish.

10 Trim off any raggedy edges while the fish is still turned inside out, then carefully turn it back right side out. The fish is ready for stuffing and baking, grilling, or roasting.

11 Inside-out fish with detached rib cage.

MATERIALS NEEDED

Newspapers

Clean worktable

Fish scaler or knife

Kitchen shears

Fish pliers or needlenose pliers

Sink or large bowl of cold water (for rinsing)

Tray to hold fish

SMALL WHOLE FRESH RED MULLET

Known as *triglia* in Italian and *rouget* in France, these small rosy-gold fish have deliciously dense, meaty, rich-tasting meat. They are usually cooked whole and if very fresh, they are often grilled without even scaling or gutting, leaving that task for the person who is eating the fish, not neglecting the succulent meat in the head including the small but tasty cheeks. Scaling a fresh-caught mullet will make its beautiful skin even redder. Red mullet may also be gutted through the gills (see "Cleaning Fish through the Gills").

Two main species of the beautiful and succulent red mullet are prized in the countries that surround the Mediterranean. They belong to the goatfish family, which have a goat beardlike barbel hanging under their chins. Red mullet (*Mullus barbatus*) are rosy with gold iridescence and a straight-fronted head. Decadently rich first-century Romans would pay sky-high prices to indulge in the morbid voyeurism of watching the color of the fish change from red to gold, to pale pink, vermillion, and blue as the fish died. Red mullet are fished in the Mediterranean, the Adriatic Sea, and the Black Sea, and off the coasts of Scandinavia and Senegal.

Striped red mullet are fished in the Mediterranean, the Black Sea, and in the Eastern Atlantic from Great Britain to Senegal, the Canary and the Azores. Of the two, striped red mullet (*M. surmuletus*) fetches the highest price. These small, narrow, fat-bodied fish have a sloping head, stripes on their first dorsal fin and often have horizontal yellow stripes on their side, though coloring varies with surroundings. Red mullet livers are a delicacy and licoricelike flavors of fennel, tarragon, and anise are classic with mullet.

PAN-DRESSING MEDIUM WHOLE FISH

Many anglers and fish lovers prefer to cook and eat small fish whole, though with scales, viscera, and often head removed. After pan-dressing, or trimming to fit in the frying pan, the cooked fish will be juicy and succulent because the meat is cooked on the bone and the connective tissue that provides rich body is intact. At the table, pull the meat away from the bone, taking care to remove any small bones.

SCALING THE FISH

1 Cover the floor area around the worktable with newspapers to catch the scales, which tend to fly everywhere. Place the fish on the worktable with its backbone away from you and its head facing your writing hand. Grasp the fish by the tail.

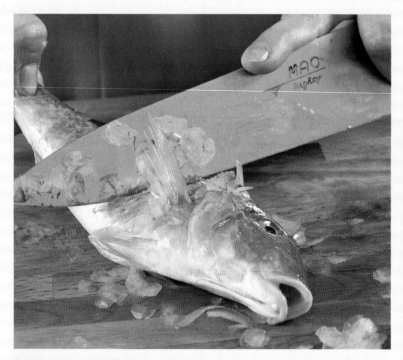

2 Scale, using a knife, scraping from the tail toward the head. Turn the fish over and scale it on the other side. Always scrape against the direction of the scales that face the head. Take extra care when scaling around the pectoral fin and the head. It's difficult to remove the scales there, but the head contains some of the tastiest meat.

3 Snip the sharp spiny dorsal fins with kitchen shears, cutting from the tail end toward the head. Cut away the pectoral fins on both sides of the fish, which lie just in back of the gill opening. The red mullet is now ready to be gutted.

GUTTING THE FISH

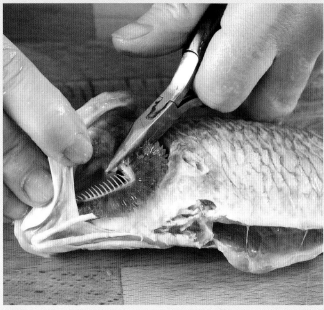

1 Turn the fish upside down and cut an opening in the belly, starting just in back of the small round anal opening and cutting forward as far as the head. Scoop out the viscera, then rinse the inside of the fish.

2 Lift up the gill cover. Grab on to the gills using fish pliers or needle-nose pliers. Pull the gills off the fish. Often the gills from both sides of the head can be removed at once. If any remain on the other side of the head, remove them too.

4 Turn the fish over and spread open the belly flaps to expose the dark kidneys. Split open the kidneys by running the knife along the backbone.

5 Fish with blood line exposed. Use a spoon to scrape out the dark red tissue then rinse under cold water.

6 Red mullet with kidneys removed and ready to cook.

MATERIALS NEEDED:

Clean cutting board

Fish filleting or utility knife

Small container for cheeks

1 Insert the knife up and down on a slight angle about halfway between the end of the gill cover and the eyes and mouth.

CUTTING FISH CHEEKS

Ask any chef what the best part of the fish is and they'll invariably reply: the cheeks. Only larger fish will have cheek muscles that are big enough to remove and cook separately. Here we remove the cheeks from a red grouper, *Epinephelus morio*—a fish with an especially large head and thick skin that is usually removed. It is fairly common and easily recognizable by its mottled brownish-red color. Meaty with few bones, grouper are sought after by sport fishermen, chefs, and consumers alike, valued for its flavor and size. Red grouper can weigh up to 50 pounds (22.7 kg), but average is 5 to 10 pounds (2.3 to 4.5 kg).

These large, solitary, predatory fish inhabit rocky, shallow warm waters in the Caribbean, the Mediterranean, and Florida and belong to the large sea bass family.

Because grouper maintains its moisture even if overcooked, it is a favorite restaurant and catering fish. Its yield is 45 percent for grouper fillet. The cheeks will weigh about 1 ounce (28 g) each.

Place the fish with its belly facing you and its tail facing your nonwriting hand. Use your fingers to locate the bowl-shaped soft cheek muscle.

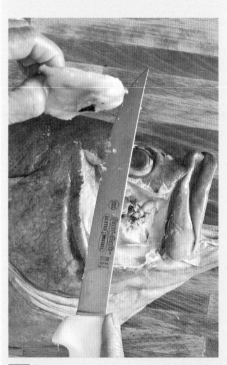

5 Sever the cheek muscle from the body of the fish.

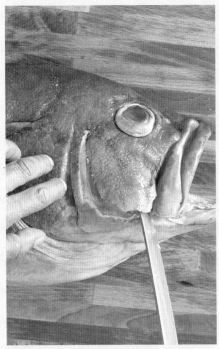

2 Make a C-shaped cut starting alongside the large grouper eye and ending at the mouth, cutting under the cheek muscle as if you were cutting under a section of grapefruit.

3 Lift up the edge of the cheek muscle.

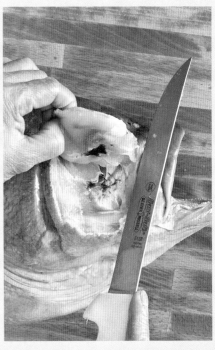

4 Continue cutting the cheek muscle away from the body leaving it attached at the top end.

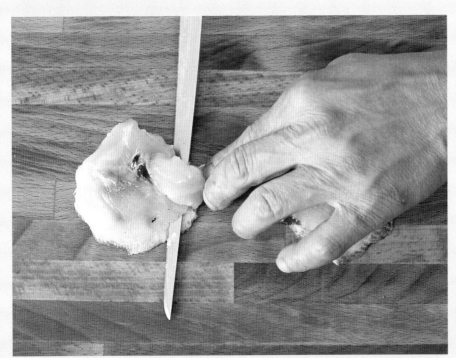

6 Turn the fish over and repeat on the other side. Now you must remove the skin. Place the cheek on the worktable with skin side down. Cut a small slit across the edge through the flesh but not through the skin. Grasp the edge of skin in your nonwriting hand. Pull the skin away while pushing against the skin with your knife, cutting the flesh away.

7 Cut all the way through the fillet, pulling the skin with one hand as you're detaching the skin with the other. Pictured: cheek muscle (without skin) ready to cook.

5:30 A.M. HONOLULU FISH AUCTION. PICTURE A LARGE ROOM FILLED WITH LARGE BIGEYE TUNA LINED UP ON PALLETS, SURROUNDED BY BIDDERS. AS THE AUCTION'S ASSISTANT GENERAL MANAGER SINCE 1979, TAKENAKA HAS BEEN ACTIVE IN TRAINING FISHERMEN AND PROCESSORS ON HOW TO HANDLE FISH FOR TOP QUALITY AND SEAFOOD SAFETY. TO INTRODUCE HAWAII SEAFOOD TO OTHER MARKETS, INCLUDING THE U.S. MAINLAND, TAKENAKA HELPED DEVELOP THE AWARD-WINNING HAWAII SEAFOOD BUYER'S GUIDE.

Brooks Takenaka, right, at the Honolulu Fish Auction

BROOKS TAKENAKA:
ASSISTANT GENERAL MANAGER OF UNITED FISHING AGENCY, HONOLULU, HAWAII

WHAT IS THE UNITED FISHING AGENCY AND CAN ANYONE VISIT?

The United Fishing Agency was incorporated in 1952 and is now Hawaii's only fish auction. Though not as large as Japan's world-famous Tsukiji Fish Market, we sell 25 to 28 million pounds (11.4 to 12.7 million kg) of fish yearly. We do allow the public to visit but keep in mind that the United Fishing Agency, aka the Honolulu Fish Auction, is a place of business and there are lots of very busy people, evaluating fish, placing bids, buying, packing, unloading, and loading fish, so stay out of the way and don't touch the fish. The auction runs six days a week. Plan on arriving about 5:30 a.m. when the auction begins, wear waterproof closed-toe footwear, and bring a jacket. It's cold on the auction floor.

HOW DOES THE AUCTION WORK?

Ideally, our captains call into the answering service to tell us what they're bringing in so our buyers can get a daily report before the auction. The boats are unloaded, then we weigh each fish and tag it with bar coding that tells when it was landed and on what vessel—each fish is fully traceable to a licensed fishing vessel. No foreign fishing vessels are allowed to unload fish in any U.S. port.

Before the auction starts, we check fish temperatures and inspect each one to be certain they meet our quality and seafood safety standards. All our fishermen have implemented standard safe fish handling procedures that have improved quality while ensuring a safe product. Our facility and seafood safety program are audited by the U.S. Food and Drug Administration yearly.

Prior to the auction, we do a tail cut, a wedge cut, and an anterior muscle coring, which facilitates quality grading and bidding. Our facilities are all refrigerated to maintain quality and seafood safety. The main buyers are wholesalers and retailers. Chefs will come to visit but normally buy their fish from wholesalers. Once a fish is auctioned, it is immediately delivered to the buyer's waiting refrigerated trucks or iced in large insulated totes for transport. A large portion of the fish stay in Hawaii, some are shipped by air to wholesalers and restaurants on the mainland, and a limited amount of our fish are exported to Japan.

WHAT ARE THE BENEFITS OF THE AUCTION SYSTEM?

The auction brings together the daily fish landings with the seafood market buyers where fair market prices are determined by open competitive bidding. The fisherman is immediately rewarded for high-quality fish and the extra attention they take to be certain fish are properly handled at sea to preserve quality and safety.

Their catch is unloaded and sold at the auction in order of arrival. By tradition, we ring a brass bell to signal the start of the auction. We start with longline-caught fish, then fish from other fishing gear types (handline, trolling, pole and line, deepwater handline). Each vessel's catch is sorted by species and size in a set pattern. Next come the tunas (bigeye, yellowfin, albacore, and skipjack), then the billfish (blue and striped marlins, spearfish, and swordfish) and associated species (mahimahi, wahoo, opah, sickle pomfrets, escolar, and thresher and mako sharks). Last we sell deepwater bottomfish including opakapaka (Hawaiian pink snapper), onaga (Hawaiian red snapper), uku (job fish), and hapuupuu (grouper).

WHAT ARE YOU DOING TO INCREASE KNOWLEDGE OF HAWAII FISH?

My colleagues and I have created the nonprofit Hawaii Seafood Council to help the longline fishing industry here. One of its first tasks was to use the United Nations Food and Agriculture Organization's Code of Conduct for Responsible Fisheries to evaluate our longline fisheries, which scored 94 percent for fishery management, operations, and research. We have one of the most intensively studied, monitored, and regulated fisheries in the world where the fishing industry, fishery scientists, and fishery managers work together to make certain that our fisheries are sustainable and that our seafood is not only good to eat, but wholesome and safe. We also co-sponsor the Hawaii Fishing and Seafood Festival, now in its fifth year as one of our most popular family-oriented events, which reflects the importance of fishing and seafood here. We launched the website (www.hawaii-seafood.org) to provide information on Hawaii's fish, our fishing industry, seafood and health, and sustainability.

WHAT FISH DO PEOPLE EAT IN HAWAII?

Fish is an essential part of Hawaii's diverse culture and food traditions. Hawaiians eat over three times the national average of fish, and some of us eat much more than our share! The most popular species here are the tunas, billfish, and other open ocean fish. We have world-class bigeye tuna, yellowfin tuna, albacore, and skipjack in Hawaii along with Pacific blue and striped marlins, spearfish and swordfish, wahoo, mahimahi, opah, deep-sea pomfrets, and escolar. Hawaiians don't eat much shark and swordfish, so these fish are mainly sold to mainland markets. We also have a limited supply of deep-sea bottomfish.

WHERE ARE THE FISH COMING FROM IN HAWAII?

Fish produced by Hawaii fishermen come from state and federal waters, while many of our longline fishing vessels operate in international waters with Honolulu the main home port. Our longline fishing vessels cannot fish within 50 miles (80.4 km) of land in Hawaii to prevent gear conflicts with smaller, shorter-range boats using handline and trolling gear. The nice thing about Hawaii is that the fish come from all sides. On the north, where the water is colder, the fish are fattier—especially good to serve raw. Our fishermen may range south closer to the equator to supply the market. Hawaii fish is sold fresh, not frozen, so our range is limited by shelf life.

WHERE DO THESE HAWAII FISH END UP?

Most of the fish stays here in the islands, where we have strong demand from locals and visitors. Some of Hawaii's fish are selling in Vancouver—a top North American seafood market, especially for sushi. Japan is another market for us, though less than before. Los Angeles buys a lot of our good-quality fish. While once the locals had the best, now the best may leave Hawaii where it can fetch a higher price.

YOU'RE NOW FISHING FOR SWORDFISH?

Swordfish is relatively new for us. In the early 90s, we discovered this significant resource while fishing for tuna, which nobody was harvesting because swordfish is not well-known in Hawaii. Our fishery now represents more than 60 percent of swordfish caught by American fishermen. Unlike the Atlantic swordfish fishery that has recently recovered from overfishing, the North Pacific stock of swordfish is in good shape and sustainably fished. Swordfish boats may be gone as long as a month. The fish are headed and gutted and kept in saltwater ice, which is much colder than freshwater ice and maintains quality quite well. Ninety-nine percent of Hawaii's swordfish ends up on the mainland.

WHAT ARE SOME DIFFERENCES IN QUALITY IN VARIOUS CATCH METHODS?

The various catch methods lead to distinct differences in fish quality. Trolling and handline fishing for tunas generally occur at shallower depths where water temperature is warmer. These fish may struggle or fight on the line, which degrades quality. Troll-caught tuna will never have the high quality or long shelf life of longline-caught tuna. With longline fishing, the hooks are set deep in the water column where temperatures are much colder. Also, the fish do not struggle as much on the line so when they are hauled in, they are in a sense prechilled—15 to 20 degrees cooler than troll-caught. Rapidly cooling tuna is the key to high quality and shelf life.

HOW DO HAWAII PEOPLE LIKE TO PREPARE THEIR FISH?

Because we have such a diversity of cultures in Hawaii, we appreciate many different species, which can be prepared so many ways. Those who come from fishing families eat all parts of the fish, like bigeye tuna head, which we grill with pink Hawaii salt. We also eat tuna collars, which is some of the better parts of the fish. As a kid, my cousins and I would fight over the heart of the tuna. A lot of fish goes to the raw market in Hawaii for native poke and Japanese sashimi and sushi. But, it's also cooked, dried, and smoked. Any form of fish is appreciated in Hawaii. We eat a lot of raw fish here in Hawaii, so quality is essential. One of the things others can learn from our people of Hawaii is . . . how to eat fish!

MATERIALS NEEDED

Clean cutting board or work surface

Kitchen shears

Filleting or utility knife

TECHNIQUE

REMOVING THE DORSAL FINS:
Many saltwater fish, including red snapper and sea bass, and freshwater fish such as perch, tilapia, and walleye pike have sharp dorsal spines that can easily puncture your skin. To remove the set of dorsal fins along the back, place the fish on a work surface with its back away from you and its head facing your nonwriting hand. Insert a sharp filleting knife just behind the head and in front of the large dorsal fin at the head end.

Cut about ½ inch (1 cm) into the flesh. Continue the cut all along the edge of the fin to its end. Turn the fish over and repeat on the other side, cutting from the tail toward the head on this side. Using your thumb and forefinger, grip the spine and pull it out—the fin and a long row of spiny bones underneath should come out cleanly in one piece. To make it easier to pull out the spines, grip them with a glove or needlenose pliers.

1 Start with a scaled and gutted fish. Place the fish with the backbone toward you and the head facing your writing hand on a clean work surface. Using kitchen shears, snip off the pectoral fins, always cutting against the direction in which the fins grow.

SLASHING FISH

Cooked whole, any fish will be juicier, more flavorful, and will lose less of its weight. Cutting diagonal slashes partway through the flesh of the fish ensures that it will cook evenly when roasted or grilled. Here we use lane snapper, *Lutjanus synagris*, a silvery-pink to reddish member of the snapper family, with short, irregular pink and yellow lines on its sides. Lane snappers live inshore over grass beds or shallow reefs; adult fish live offshore off wrecks and on reefs. It is a close cousin to the more glamorous and visually striking true American red snapper and similar to the mutton snapper, *L. analis*, and the mangrove snapper, *L. griseus*.

5 Turn the fish over so that its backbone is facing away from you and its head facing your nonwriting hand. Make a deep diagonal cut about two-thirds of the way through the flesh, starting just behind the head and cutting from the backbone toward the belly.

2 Snip off the pelvic fin on the belly of the fish.

3 Snip off the dorsal fins on the backbone, cutting from the tail end toward the head (taking care to avoid the sharp spines).

4 Snip off the anal fin. Trim the tail, leaving about 1 inch (2.5 cm).

6 Make a slightly shallower cut, parallel to the first one, approximately 1 inch (2.5 cm) away from the first cut.

7 Repeat, making a third cut that is shallower than the second cut. Flip the fish over, so that its backbone is facing toward you and its head is facing your nonwriting hand. Make the same three cuts on the opposite side. The fish is now ready for cooking.

CUTTING SWORDFISH CHOPS

Here we cut two chops from the collar of a headed and gutted swordfish, a part usually discarded by wholesalers. New York chef David Burke actually trademarked this "swordfish chop" but later gave up the trademark partly because so many chefs had copied the high-priced limited cut. Other chefs serve a similar cut as prime rib of swordfish. A single chop weighs about 1 pound (450 g) with a long bone, part of the collarbone (not a rib bone), along the chop, and is 3 to 4 inches (7.5 to 10 cm) thick. In shape and weight, this cut indeed mimics prime rib.

A single species of swordfish, *Xiphias gladius*, roams the temperate and tropical waters of Earth. The solitary swimmer may reach 15 feet (4.5 m) long, and has a huge sword protruding from the front of its head that itself may be as much as 5 feet (1.5 m) long. Although stocks have recovered, swordfish's popularity has not recovered since the chefs' campaign started in 1998 to "Give Swordfish a Break," to help North Atlantic stocks recover. At the time, Pacific swordfish were relatively abundant, but all swordfish were included in the campaign.

Swordfish often appeals to those who don't like fish, because of its dense steaklike texture and mild flavor.

Fish markets buy sections of swordfish called "wheels" that may be cut into whole round, half, or quarter-round steaks depending on the size of the fish. Small swordfish are headed and gutted and sold as "logs." Whole swordfish are mostly white with colored bands of blue to blue-violet running lengthwise across the body. They can weigh more than 1,000 pounds (454 kg), though 50 to 200 pounds (22.7 to 90.8 kg) is more common. Their flesh ranges in color from cream to ivory to pinkish-orange and is moderately high in oil with firm and meaty, though slightly mealy, texture. Fillet yield is 80 percent from whole round steaks. Always consider buying swordfish from colder waters—they are less subject to parasites.

1 You'll be removing the excess skin and flesh from the swordfish collar, exposing the "rib bone," actually a bone that surrounds the gill opening, and cutting the "steak" portion from the meat at the head end. Using your nonwriting hand, hold down the body of the fish to steady it. Insert the knife underneath the collarbone on the body side of the collar. The bone begins just past the belly section, about 1 inch (2.5 cm) below the main portion of the meat, cutting from the belly toward the head. Slice off a strip about a ½ inch (1 cm) thick to trim the outside of the fish.

3 Grasping the belly section of the swordfish in your nonwriting hand, make a second cut parallel to the first one. Then cut across so that the two cuts meet. This severs the excess belly meat.

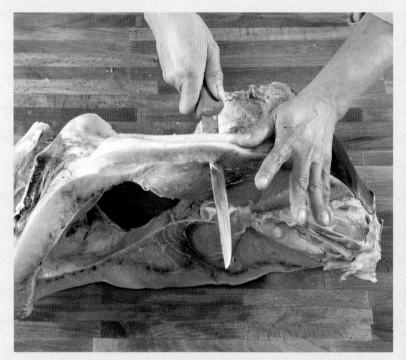

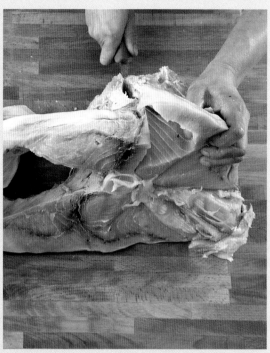

2 Pull away the strip without cutting it off. Find the place just above the darker portion that encloses the main meat from the belly meat. Grasping the attached bone, slice from the backbone to the edge of the collar, perpendicular to the body.

4 Turn the fish over so its backbone faces your writing hand. Insert the knife under the collarbone. Cut underneath the bone until just past the dark red connective tissue that encloses the main portion of the meat.

5 Cut away the belly portion, as on the first side.

6 Turn the head portion so that the collarbone "wings" are facing toward you and the backbone is on the work surface. Insert the knife along the near side of the backbone. Cut straight down all the way through the flesh.

7 Cut all the way through the meat pulling, away the portion that will become the chop. Sever the "chop" from the head.

10 Cut the chop away from the bones.

11 Turn the chop so that the head end faces your writing hand and the backbone is toward you, grasping the bone in your nonwriting hand. Insert your knife at the end of the chop bone where it meets the main portion of the meat. Slice underneath the connective tissue on the outer edge. Cut off the connective tissue.

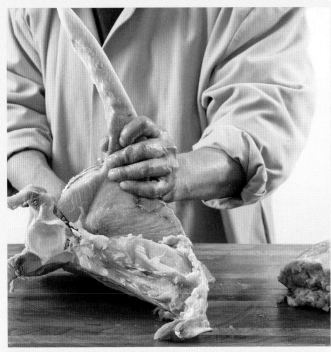

8 Grasp the chop portion just behind the bone with your nonwriting hand to steady it. Insert your knife next to the backbone to trim away the chop.

9 Continue cutting between the main portion of the meat and the bones.

12 Grasping the bone with your nonwriting hand, turn the chop so that its skin is against the work surface. Cut a slice about ¾ inch (2 cm) thick from the head end to make an even edge.

13 With your knife parallel to the meat, trim the connective tissue off the chop at the backbone side. Cut away the connective tissue.

14 Turn the chop over so that its skin side is up. Grasp the end of the bone in your nonwriting hand. Insert the knife under the skin of the chop bone.

15 Cut off the skin from the chop bone and insert the knife under the skin of the body. Cut off the skin.

16 Holding the chop in your nonwriting hand with the bone down and facing away from you, cut off the meat on either side of the bone.

17 Finished swordfish chop. Repeat the steps on the other side of the fish for the second chop.

MATERIALS NEEDED

Large, clean work surface

Heavy filleting knife or chef's knife

Tray to store the steaks

CUTTING FISH STEAKS FROM HALIBUT

Just like a beef steak, a fish steak is cut straight through the body of a large fish. The huge diamond-shaped halibut, *Hippoglossus stenolepis*, is the largest of all flatfish and among the largest fish in the sea. Giant Pacific fish, called barn door halibut, can reach over 8 feet (2.4 m) in length and over 5 feet (1.5 m) wide, though 5 pounds (2.3 kg) to 100 (45.4 kg) is average. Small fish are called chicken halibut; large adults are known as whales. Halibut is an important and valuable commercial fishery in the cold northern waters of both the North American Atlantic and Pacific coasts. The males weigh up to about 60 pounds (27.2 kg); the females are much heavier at up to 600 pounds (272.4 kg). Atlantic halibut, *H. hippoglossus*, are caught close to shore from Labrador to Maine and are now being farmed.

Halibut have a large mouth, a forked tail, dark green-brown skin on their upper side, and gray-white skin below. Like other flatfish, halibut are bottom dwellers and strong swimmers. Most halibut remain in roughly the same area, but they may swim thousands of miles. Eighty percent of Pacific halibut comes from Alaska where they are in peak season from April through October.

The halibut's snow-white meat is fine textured, dense, and has few bones. Because it has such lean meat, it is important not to overcook halibut. Its dark upper side skin is edible though often removed. Its mild adaptable flavor and high nutritional value make halibut a chef's favorite. Pacific halibut is generally softer in texture than Atlantic halibut. Yield for halibut is quite high at 50 to 60 percent. If your halibut is head-on, make sure to remove the cheeks as they are a delicacy (see "Cutting Fish Cheeks").

TECHNIQUE

CUTTING A LARGE FLATFISH INTO TRANCHES: Large flatfish such as halibut and turbot may be portioned into tranches, a term that is derived from the French word for slice. Place the gutted flatfish dark side up on a clean cutting board and trim off the frilly edge, also called the skirt, around the edges and the tail.

With a heavy chef's knife, cut down the length of the backbone using the darker lateral line in the center as a guide. Use a meat cleaver to help cut through the heaviest bones. Ideally, the backbone of the fish will be split in half so each portion gets some of the bone, which helps keep it intact.

Cut crosswise to make squarish portions, adjusting the width of the cut to allow for changes in thickness. The tail-end tranche will be triangular in shape; the other cuts will be roughly rectangular.

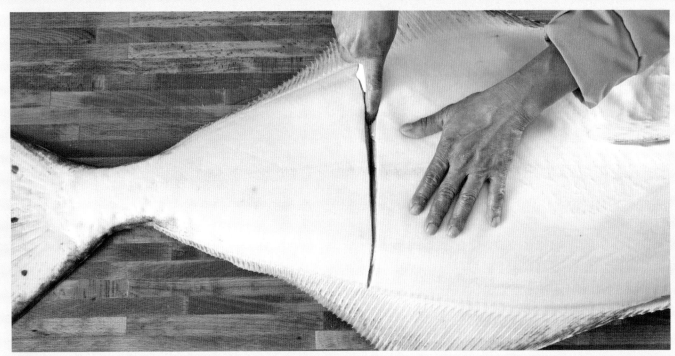

1 Place the halibut on a clean work surface with its lower light side up and its head facing your nonwriting hand. Insert the knife into the edge of the fish, about two-thirds of the way down its length toward the tail cutting into the flesh of the fish beyond the wavy fins. Cut toward yourself, cutting deeply all the way through the fish and its backbone.

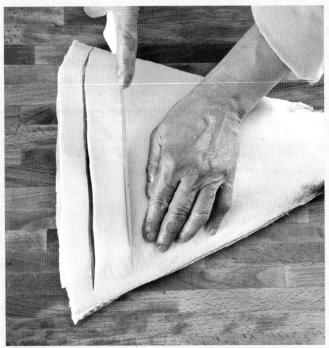

4 Starting about ½ inch (1 cm) from the edge of the fish, insert the knife and make a slice across the width of the fish about 1 inch (2.5 cm) thick, cutting toward yourself. Repeat with the second cut, placing it about 1 inch (2.5 cm) away from the first slice.

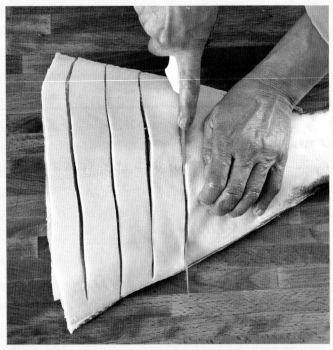

5 Continue making parallel cuts through the fish. As you get closer to the tail and the flesh gets thinner, make the cuts farther apart. For this fish, we'll end up with five steaks.

2 Now cut away the tail end of the fish from the main body. Put the body of the fish aside and reserve for another use.

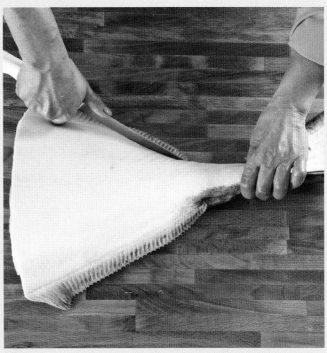

3 Rotate the fish so its tail faces your nonwriting hand. Grasp the thinner part of the fish between the tail and the body in your hand. Working from the tail end toward the front of the fish, cut away the wavy fins on either side.

6 Sever the halibut steaks from the fish by cutting through the end that is attached.

I STILL REMEMBER THE BEST SMOKED SALMON I'VE EVER TASTED—IT CAME FROM H. FORMAN & SON, A HISTORIC LONDON SMOKEHOUSE, THE LAST OF THE GREAT SMOKED FISH COMPANIES.

LANCE FORMAN:
MANAGING DIRECTOR OF
H. FORMAN & SON, LONDON.

That salmon forever set my benchmark for smoked salmon—silky smooth, with dense flesh, deep color, and a subtle smoke flavor that enhanced the flavor of the wild salmon itself. I spoke to Lance Forman, managing director of this fourth-generation family fish smokehouse.

Forman was president of the Cambridge Union and was later appointed special adviser to the Secretary of State for Trade and Industry. He has been with Forman's since 1994, where he pioneered the company's growth in specialty British food with his launch of Forman and Field. His battle with former mayor of London over the compulsory purchase of the Forman's factory led to the development of a new premises, venue, and restaurant—Forman's Fish Island—in record-breaking speed.

YOUR COMPANY IS ONE OF THE HISTORIC LONDON JEWISH FISH SMOKEHOUSES. WHAT ARE THE ORIGINS OF FORMAN'S?
My great-grandfather Aaron Forman, known as Harry, came from Odessa, Ukraine, and settled in the East End of London, then a center for Jewish immigration, and founded Forman's in 1905. Today Forman's is the world's leading supplier of smoked Scottish wild salmon. Until the 1970s, there were still about a dozen fish smokers in the area, including Barnett's of Frying Pan Alley, but now we're the only one left.

Hanging salmon from hooks for smoking at Forman's

FORMAN'S IS KNOWN FOR ITS LONDON-CURE SALMON. IS LONDON CURE THE SAME AS SCOTTISH SMOKED SALMON?

The mild London cure developed as immigrant Jewish fish-curers realized they could buy fresh-caught salmon from Scotland instead of relying on the barrels of salted fish they had been importing from the Baltic region. At first, only locals bought their fish, but as they developed the lighter London cure using fresh Scottish salmon, it began to be served in the best restaurants and hotels. It didn't take long for canny Scottish smokers to adapt their own traditional highly smoked peat-fired fish to the London cure.

YOU USE FARMED SALMON FOR THE MAJORITY OF YOUR SMOKING. WHAT MAKES YOUR FISH DIFFERENT?

The most important thing of all is that the fish be fresh. Our fish is no more than 48 hours out of the water, so it's firm with good texture. Industrial salmon smokers fillet their fish mechanically, so they have to wait a few days until the fish is out of rigor mortis. We start filleting as soon as the fish arrive. About 20 percent of the salmon we smoke is wild Scottish, which we hang from a cord to smoke in the traditional way, concentrating the flavor and thereby shrinking the weight of the fish. We smoke our farmed salmon the same way and also on racks where they gently dry and smoke over twenty-four hours.

WHAT HAPPENS TO THE FISH ONCE THEY ARRIVE?

The fish arrive daily from Scotland and we start work at 4 a.m. First we grade the fish and check the quality on arrival. We do everything by hand: filleting, pulling out the pin bones, tying fish for hanging, rubbing the fish with coarse salt, trimming off the *pellicle*—the crust that forms on smoked fish. We leave the fish on the bone, drying it in the kiln for eight to ten hours. Industrial operations remove the belly bones and pin bones before smoking, but just as a steak cooked on the bone will be juicier, so is our fish. We're much more like a kitchen than a normal factory. We don't even start the process until we get an order and almost always hand-carve the fish and send it to customers the same day it leaves the kiln.

WHAT DO YOU USE TO SMOKE YOUR SALMON?

Our fish contains only about 3 percent salt and no sugar, which is often added by commercial smokers to neutralize the large amount of salt their fish contains—up to 5 percent. We smoke lightly in oak smoke created by friction burning whole oak logs; it is light because we want people to taste the fish first, not the smoke. Our fish doesn't have a long shelf life—it's best eaten within one week, though it does take well to freezing.

DO YOU USE FROZEN FISH?

By law, wild salmon must be frozen because the cold-smoking process we use doesn't raise the temperature of the fish enough to kill any parasites, not that parasites are found in wild Scottish salmon, but this is a legal precaution. The process of defrosting actually enhances the fish because the flesh becomes more porous and draws in the smoke, giving it a lovely even flavor.

HOW IS INEXPENSIVE COMMERCIAL SMOKED SALMON PRODUCED?

Along with the growth of aqua-farmed salmon, supermarkets have pressured their suppliers to find cheaper sources for fish, such as heavily subsidized Norwegian farmed salmon, and faster ways of production, such as brining, which pumps up weight and gives the fish longer shelf life, though yielding a much saltier product with compromised texture. Some processors don't smoke the fish at all; they just spray it with smoke flavoring.

SLICING SMOKED SALMON BY HAND IS BECOMING A LOST ART. DO YOU SLICE BY HAND?

We slice by hand from the head downward after first trimming the smoked side, also by hand. It takes only a few minutes for our expert slicers to trim, pull out the thirty-two pin bones, and lateral slice a 3-pound (1.4-kg) side. Indeed one of our slicers recently set the Guinness World Record for hand-slicing smoked salmon. Every part of the fish finds a market, from the heads to the bones and the pellicle trimmings, which are great for making patés.

FORMAN'S RECENTLY MOVED. WHY?

We lost our last location (we've only had four locations in 105 years of business, all located in the East End) due to eminent domain—the City of London needed our land for the 2012 Olympic stadium. Our new plant is the closest building to the Olympics site and includes a restaurant where people can taste our smoked salmon and seasonal British foods.

1 Using your nonwriting hand grasp the head of the fish by placing your thumb inside the gill cover to get a good grip on the head and make a deep diagonal cut behind the fin and behind the collarbone to sever the head.

2 Place your nonwriting hand flat on the fish, close to the head end. Insert your knife just above the backbone at the head end. Cut toward the tail, sliding the knife alongside the bones and angling it toward the bones rather than toward the flesh so as not to cut into the flesh. Cut about one-third of the body width on this round.

FILLETING SALMON

Here we fillet a farmed Atlantic salmon, only because wild salmon was not in season at the time. There are enormous environmental problems with underwater mega-farms; it's difficult to imagine that we can turn back the clock to the days when all salmon was wild. Environmentally conscious salmon farmers such as Cooke Aquaculture in New Brunswick, Canada, and Scotland's Loch Duart salmon (which won The Queen's Award for Enterprise in the International Trade category in 2008) are working to upgrade the environmental and quality standards for salmon fishing worldwide in the future. There must be a sustainable solution to the market demand.

Most salmon come to the market already gutted, but if you catch your own it is not necessary to gut the fish before filleting. While many environmentalists recommend that we eschew farmed salmon and buy only wild salmon, a large majority of salmon is farmed.

The quality of wild salmon is directly related to the length the river it must swim to reach its spawning grounds. The higher its oil content, the better its flavor. The best wild salmon are troll-caught, gill-bled, and chilled onboard. For all salmon, the richest and fattiest part is the belly; the leanest part is the tail.

To begin, place the salmon with its backbone toward you and its head toward your writing hand.

3 Reverse directions. Grasp the free end of the fish in your nonwriting hand and continue cutting from the tail end toward the head. This time, cut about halfway through the body.

4 Once the fillet has been cut away to the head, pull the near-fillet away with your nonwriting hand. Cut again from the head to the tail, this time cutting through the belly bones and all across the width of the fish.

6 Flip the fish so its head faces your nonwriting hand with its backbone still up. Insert the knife just above the backbone in front of the tail. Using your nonwriting hand to steady the fish, cut from the tail end of the fish. Cut about 2 inches (5 cm) deep (or about one-third of the body width) on this round.

5 Remove the top fillet and trim away the dorsal fin and surrounding bones on the top edge of the fillet.

7 Reverse directions. Grasp the free end of the fillet with your nonwriting hand and cut all the way through the fish from the backbone to the belly. Remove the top fillet and trim away the white fatty bony belly section.

8 Firmly grasping the free end of the fillet with your nonwriting hand, continue to cut through the fish to the tail. The point of your knife should poke through the belly. Remove the second fillet and trim away the dorsal fin and surrounding bones on the top edge of the fillet.

MATERIALS NEEDED:

Clean cutting board or work surface

Heavy filleting or chef's knife

Needlenose pliers or fish pliers

Tray to store the steaks

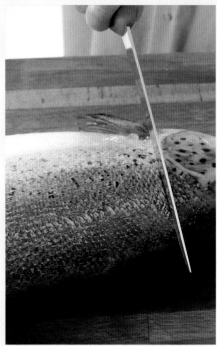

1 To cut steaks from a salmon, place the salmon on the work surface with its head facing your nonwriting hand and its backbone away from you.

CUTTING FISH STEAKS FROM SALMON

A fish steak will be juicier and have less weight loss than a fillet, and because it contains bones, skin, and connective tissue—all of which contribute to flavor and richness of texture. In this technique, we cut salmon steaks. (See "Boning Fish Steak and Making Fish Roulade" to learn how to make a beautiful roulade from a salmon steak, suitable for the fanciest meal.)

4 Make a second cut that is about the same thickness. Continue making slices throughout the length of the fish. To make portions of equal weight, cut thinner slices from the thickest part of the fish.

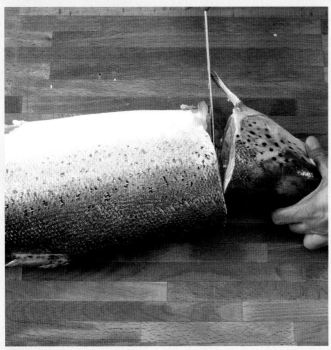

2 Cut all the way through the fish to sever the head. Remove the head.

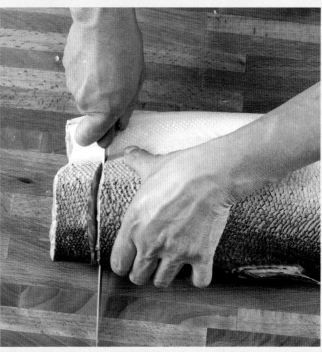

3 Turn the fish over so its head faces your writing hand with its backbone still away from you. Grasp the body of the fish with your nonwriting hand over the backbone to steady it. Cut through the thickest portion of the fish, leaving the steaks attached at the belly end.

5 After you slice the steaks, return to the first one and cut all the way through at the belly end to sever the steaks.

6 Prepared salmon steaks. Each contains pin bones that should be removed, located above the backbone and at a 45-degree angle to the center line. Each ring of flesh contains one pin bone. Remove them using fish pliers or needlenose pliers (see "Removing Pin Bones from Round Fish").

MATERIALS NEEDED:

Clean cutting board or work surface

Needlenose pliers or fish pliers

Filleting knife or sharp paring knife

Kitchen string or natural twine

Tray to store roulade

BONING FISH STEAK AND MAKING FISH ROULADE

Here we bone a salmon steak and transform it into a round of fish, known as a *roulade* (from the French). Many recipes for roulade consist of fish fillet that is rolled up with a filling to make a pinwheel shape. The roulade is made from a single salmon steak that is boned and cut in a special way. The rosy salmon meat ends up enclosed in a ring of silvery skin tied with kitchen string, ready to be poached, roasted, grilled, or sautéed and served at an elegant meal.

1 Each steak will contain pin bones that must be removed, located above the backbone and at a 45-degree angle to the center line.

4 Trim off the flesh from the tail portion, leaving the skin attached.

2 To remove the center bone from a salmon or cod steak, lay the steak flat on a clean cutting board, holding it in place with your nonwriting hand with the belly end facing you. Insert the tip of a sharp knife just under the skin on the near side of the center bone. Cut downward following the shape of the bone.

3 Continue the cut past the bone on the inner side of the stomach opening, cutting between the flesh and the belly opening to remove the membrane.

5 Partially trimmed salmon steak.

6 Turn the fish steak over, belly section toward you. Insert the knife just under the skin on the near side of the salmon steak, cutting from the backbone to the center bone. Cut downward, following the shape of the bone, keeping the blade flat. Separate the inner membrane from the flesh.

7 Salmon steak with backbone section cut free.

8 Holding the backbone section in your nonwriting hand, cut it away from the steak just under the skin.

12 Curl the two ends of the salmon around the inner side of the fillet.

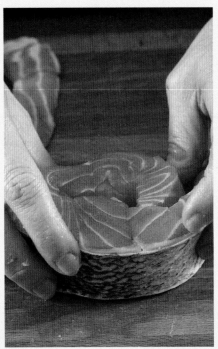

13 Wrap the outer section of salmon with its skin around the salmon fillet.

14 Trim the end of the second belly flap so that it is just long enough to overlap the round. Wrap the free end around the fish to form a neat, rounded shape.

9 Place the salmon skin side down, opening it up on the work surface. Insert the knife between the meat and the skin and cut from the center to the belly edge on one side only.

10 Turn the salmon steak with its skin on the work surface, and trim off the end of the salmon that is still attached to the skin. Cut a flap from underneath the belly section.

11 Place the salmon fillet portion alongside the salmon section attached to its skin.

15 Tie a length of twine or kitchen string around the center of the roulade. Pull the ends of the string to make a compact round shape.

16 Completed fish roulade.

MATERIALS NEEDED:

Clean cutting board or work surface

Kitchen shears

Heavy filleting knife or chef's knife

Spoon (optional)

Tray to store the steaks

CUTTING FISH STEAKS FROM COD

Cod is a lean and flaky fish that cooks best in steak form—the skin and bones hold the fish together, adding rich body and juiciness to a fish that can easily flake apart and become dry. Here, we show how to cut steaks from a scaled, headed, and gutted Atlantic cod.

TRIMMING THE FINS

1 Place the fish with its head end facing your nonwriting hand.

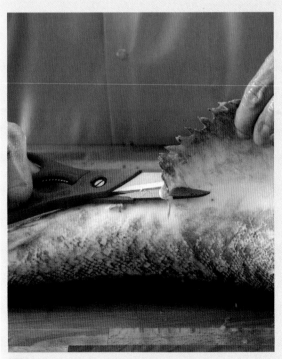

3 Lift up the forward dorsal fins and snip off.

2 Lift up the dorsal fins along its backbone and snip off, cutting from the tail end to the head.

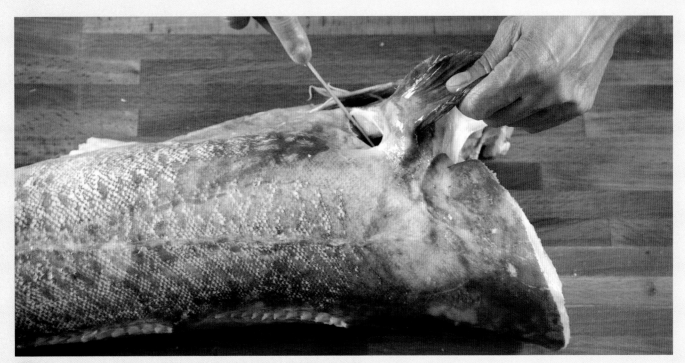

4 Lift up the pectoral fin and cut it away from its base. Repeat on the other side.

TRIMMING THE HEAD AND BELLY

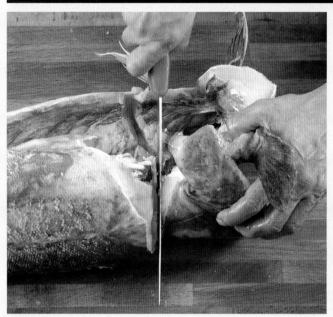

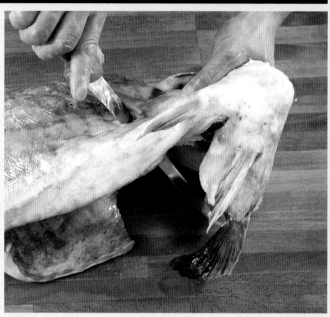

1 Turn the fish over so its belly faces up. Make a cut about 2 inches (5 cm) into the fish on both sides of the belly just behind the pectoral fins. Now cut through the fish (including the backbone) using the first cut as a guideline. Leave the front portion still attached.

2 Grasp the front portion with your nonwriting hand. Insert the knife just behind the cut and slice off the belly flap. Repeat on the other side of the fish.

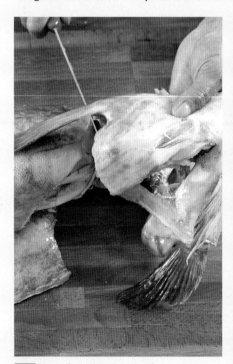

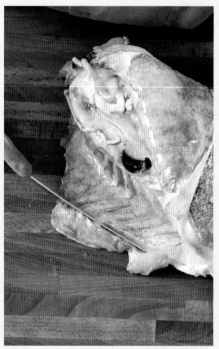

3 Now slice off the front portion.

4 Turn the fish so its head faces your writing hand and so its backbone faces you. Trim the edges of the belly.

5 Turn the fish over and trim the belly on the other side.

REMOVING THE VISCERA

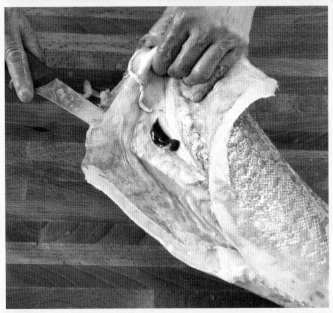

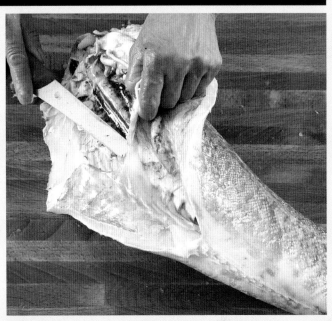

1 There is a tough membrane that encloses the viscera section along with the cod's inflatable swim bladder. Grasp the head end of the fish in your nonwriting hand and insert the knife just under the membrane to cut it away.

2 Using your nonwriting hand, lift up the free end of the membrane, continuing to cut until you have removed it, exposing the backbone.

CUTTING FISH STEAKS

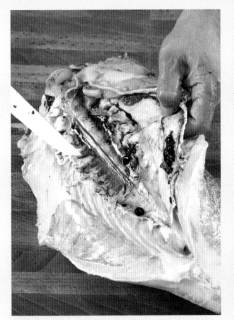

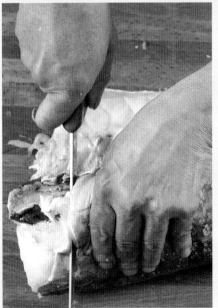

3 Open the fish from the belly side, exposing the backbone and kidneys. Slit open the kidneys, exposing the dark red tissue, then scrape it away using your fingers or a spoon. Rinse the fish under cold water.

1 Turn the fish so that its head end faces your writing hand and its belly is toward you. Using your nonwriting hand grasp the free end of the belly to steady it. Insert the knife about 1 inch (2.5 cm) behind the head end.

2 Slice off the first steak. Continue cutting off fish steaks about 1 inch (2.5 cm) thick. Note that the first cut will be smaller and bonier than subsequent cuts.

*Aglaia Kremezi shares her love
of fresh, seasonal Greek food*

AGLAIA KREMEZI:
GREEK CULINARY AUTHORITY, AUTHOR, AND JOURNALIST

I attended Greek culinary authority Aglaia Kremezi's Kea Artisanal, a one-week cooking course held on the Greek Cycladic island of Kea, where she and her husband make their home. Kremezi has written regularly for the *Los Angeles Times, Gourmet* magazine, *BBC Good Food* magazine, *Bon Appetit, Food and Wine*, and other publications in Greece and the United States and is the author of several books, including a Julia Child award winner. Kremezi studies the history of ancient Greek and Mediterranean cuisines and has presented papers at the Oxford Symposium on Food and Cookery. She is a consultant for Molyvos, the first upscale Greek restaurant in New York, which garnered three stars from the *New York Times.*

WHAT ARE YOUR FAVORITE KINDS OF FISH AND SHELLFISH?

I love whatever extremely fresh fish—often still moving—the boats bring to our port. There is a Greek saying: The best fish is the freshest fish. For example, yesterday I got four wonderful firm-fleshed weevers (*drakena* in Greek, from "dragon" because of its venomous spines) and a few tiny pipers, with which I made a delicious *psaro-hortosoupa* (fish and vegetable soup)

the way my mother used to make it. It is quite time-consuming as it involves cooking the heads and bones separately for the stock, then passing everything through two or three different sieves and then adding sautéed garlic, onion, some potatoes, and finally lemon, olive oil, and the fish fillets.

I love sea urchins, but only if they are just taken out of the sea, and simply drizzled with lemon.

WHAT KIND OF CHANGES HAVE YOU SEEN IN TASTE AND AVAILABILITY OF SEAFOOD IN YOUR LIFE?

My father used to be the head of the legal department of the Piraeus Port Authority (he actually wrote the laws for the creation of the country's main port, in the 1930s) so he had access to *great* fish, which my mother served at least twice a week. But as most kids, neither I nor my sister appreciated it. Later, when I started to cook, I had my favorite fishmonger in downtown Athens, and I spent quite a bit of money to get good fish, which wasn't always available. I was really thrilled when farm-raised sea breams started to be accessible.

ARE THERE ANY SPECIES THAT YOU USED TO EAT AND CAN'T FIND ANYMORE?

Skaros, a kind of Mediterranean parrot fish (*Euscarus cretensis*), was supposed to be grilled unscaled and ungutted, as its flavor was enhanced from its innards, which we mashed together with olive oil and lemon to make a delicious dark sauce. It was always hard to find, but I haven't seen it for ages.

WHAT IS THE GREEK PHILOSOPHY IN COOKING FISH?

As with *all* the flavorful seasonal ingredients, fish is simply grilled, fried, or boiled, and served with a dressing of olive oil and lemon. We are not fond of elaborate fish dishes.

ARE THERE ANY TRADITIONAL GREEK FISH DISHES USING RAW PRODUCT? HOW ABOUT SALTED FISH OR PICKLED FISH?

Very fresh anchovies and sardines are briefly marinated in vinegar or lemon juice, and served dressed with chopped garlic and olive oil.

CAN YOU TALK ABOUT TARAMA AND BOTTARGA AND ITS PLACE IN GREEK CUISINE?

Avgotaraho (the Greek *bottarga*—but the term comes from the word *avgotaraho*) preserved fish in ancient Greek is the salted and smoked roe of gray mullet, prepared in Messolongi, on the eastern part of the mainland. It always was a really precious and expensive delicacy, far better than any other bottarga you will find. Tarama is hake roe (I think), imported to Greece from Northern Europe, in order to make our traditional salad. The white, and not the pink, kind is the best.

MATERIALS NEEDED:

Sink or large bowl of cold water (for rinsing)

Paper towels

Kitchen shears or small paring knife

Small spoon (optional)

Clean cutting board or work surface

Tray to store fish

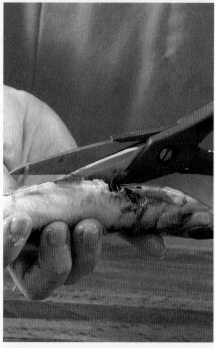

1 Hold a fish in your nonwriting hand. Use kitchen shears or a small paring knife to cut the belly open, slitting from the head end toward the tail. Using your fingers or a small spoon, remove the viscera from inside the belly.

DEBONING SMALL BONY FISH

Here we remove the backbone and attached rib bones from fresh sardines. In the UK, this old-time technique is called *spatchcock*, an eighteenth-century term that is thought to be of Irish origin, or perhaps an abbreviation of *dispatch cock* in which the bird is split down the back, flattened, and grilled. To muddy the waters, the nearly identical word *spitchcock* is an obsolete British culinary term used for grilled eel. Whether the method and its name come from chickens or eels, it is an easy way to remove the fine and all too abundant bones from small, oily fish such as sardines, small mackerel, and herring.

Sardines, *Sardina pilchardus*, are small, silvery fish with green backs and yellow sides, fine, soft skin, and rich flesh. True sardines come from Europe where young sardines are hugely popular in Portugal, Spain, Italy, Greece, France, and Turkey. Larger sardines are most common in Northern Europe. In the UK, *sardine* refers to young fish and *pilchard* to older fish. Sardines are often grilled, especially over natural hardwood charcoal, because their soft, dark, rather oily flesh benefits by cooking over direct heat.

Because they are extremely perishable, fresh sardines are seasonal, usually local, served in summer near the coasts where they're harvested. Its yield is 45 to 50 percent.

To begin, rinse the sardines under cold water and pat dry.

4 Turn the fish over and gently pull the backbone away from the flesh, working from the head end toward the tail.

2 Open the fish like a book and place it skin side up on a clean cutting board.

3 Press down firmly on the backbone with your thumb, near the head. Press down along the whole length of the backbone.

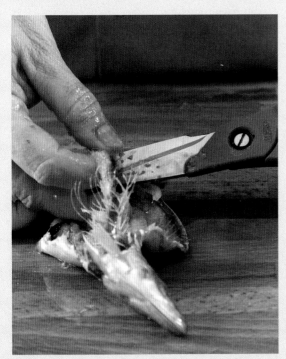

5 Using kitchen shears, snip off the backbone at the tail end. Use your fingers to pull out the bones along the sides.

6 Rinse the fish and pat dry. The sardines are ready for cooking.

Bringing in an albacore tuna
caught with pole and line

IN 2004 NATALIE WEBSTER CO-FOUNDED THE AMERICAN ALBACORE FISHING ASSOCIATION TO EDUCATE CONSUMERS ABOUT THE DOMESTIC POLE-AND-TROLL ALBACORE FISHERY, ITS FAMILIES, AND PRODUCTS. AFTER A FIVE-YEAR PROCESS, THIS TUNA FISHERY BECAME THE FIRST IN THE WORLD TO BE MARINE STEWARDSHIP COUNCIL—CERTIFIED.

NATALIE WEBSTER:
DIRECTOR OF OPERATIONS FOR AMERICAN ALBACORE FISHING ASSOCIATION AND MEMBER OF A FIFTH-GENERATION ALBACORE TUNA FISHING FAMILY

Natalie Webster was born in San Diego, California, which from the early 1900s up until the mid-80s, was considered the tuna fishing capital of the world. Both her father and grandfather were pole and troll tuna fishermen in San Diego. Her husband, Jack Webster, also works in this artisanal fishery. In the 80s when the tuna fishery in San Diego was affected by the dolphin-safe mandate, most tuna vessels went to foreign flags, harvesting and unloading in foreign countries for canning and processing. The United States soon followed.

HOW DID YOUR FAMILY GET INTO TUNA FISHING?

My husband, Jack, is a pole-and-troll albacore fisherman as were both my father and grandfather. After my dad married my mother, my grandfather put my dad on a boat to learn to fish for albacore. My grandfather on my mother's side immigrated to Massachusetts, bringing along his knowledge of traditional Portuguese albacore tuna fishing. He later moved to California where he worked with Portuguese and Italian fishermen.

Eight other fishing families, Jack, and I co-founded the nonprofit American Albacore Fishing Association to revitalize an almost-lost local and sustainable fishery. We banded together with five traditional fishing families to create American Tuna, our artisanal company that markets whole frozen and canned albacore tuna from the only pole-and-line MSC-certified albacore

If we don't take care of the fish, our children and grandchildren won't have any wild seafood to eat and our fishing families won't be able to earn a living.

A haul of smaller hand-caught albacore tuna

WHAT MAKES YOUR CANNED TUNA WORTH THE EXTRA COST?

Our tuna goes into the can raw, where it is cooked in its own natural juices. Its taste and juiciness are phenomenal and the yield is high because each can contains a whole slice of tuna. We add nothing but salt (or no salt at all), so all the beneficial natural fish oils remain in the can. Commercial canners can older, larger tuna, which are higher in mercury. The tuna itself is frozen, defrosted, and cooked several times in processing and usually contains soy sauce, broth, and other fillers. The North Pacific albacore that we harvest feed on anchovies and sardines so they are extremely fatty. Our canned tuna contains an amazing ten times the amount of omega-3s as most brands—don't throw out that oil!

IS THE NORTH PACIFIC ALBACORE TUNA FISHERY SUSTAINABLE?

Subadult fish—only 12 to 25 pounds (5.4 to 11.4 kg)—that swim near the surface are captured one at a time using nothing more than bait, pole, and troll. With zero bycatch and zero impact on the environment, marine life, the ocean floor, the reef, or any animals such as turtles, the fishery is sustainable. Commercial albacore fishing targets larger adult fish (70 to 80 pounds [31.8 to 36.3 kg]) using longlines as much as 30 miles (48.3 km) in length. These fish often die on the hook; our fish are alive until they're brought on deck and frozen. Other vessels use purse seines, which are indiscriminate, killing baby fish, capturing unwanted species, and ultimately harming the future of these fish because none are left behind for the next generation.

WHY SHOULD WE WORRY ABOUT ILLEGALLY CAUGHT TUNA?

Illegal, unregulated, unreported fish: Without traceability nobody knows whether the fish was caught using illegal drift nets, which harm our oceans and harm our fishermen and their families, because these fish are sold at less-than-market value. Luckily for us, as of 2009, the European Union and the UK now require a catch certificate showing where and how that fish was caught.

WHAT CAN WE LEARN FROM TUNA FISHING TRADITION?

We've had multiple generations on the ocean teaching our offspring how to fish for albacore. Our fishermen travel up to 1,000 miles (1,609 km) offshore, though normally they stay within the 200-mile (322 km) Exclusive Economic Zone. In the summer months off the coasts of Oregon and Washington, they'll experience tremendous gale force winds. These are not big boats. Our captains must judge the weather and

WHAT IS THE JOB OF THE CAPTAIN?

The captain/owner is port engineer, chief engineer, navigator, deck boss, doctor on board, fish finder, business manager, and financier. (Although we don't have any female captains, many wives crew for their husbands.) Most important, he takes the responsibility for the lives under his care: Good decisions make the difference between life and death.

HOW CAN CONSUMERS HELP?

Most people don't even know that this pole-and-line albacore fishery exists. If we don't take care of the fish, our children and grandchildren won't have any wild seafood to eat and our fishing families won't be able

TIP

With its large size and need to move quickly, tuna have a different bone structure than other fish: a set of four strips of bones radiate out from the central spine bone facing north, south, east, and west, so you will be removing four loin sections from the fish. Because the fish is so large, it is difficult to move it around and special techniques are used for filleting. In this case, we move the tuna as we cut it. For larger fish, once the top two loins have been removed, the tail portion is lifted up and the bottom loins are removed by chipping away at the lower strip of bones (facing "south"). When cutting tuna, it's especially important to cut with a single, smooth stroke to avoid breaking up the delicate and valuable flesh.

MATERIALS NEEDED

Large, clean work surface

Heavy filleting knife (preferably a fish filleting knife)

Large tray to hold the loins

CUTTING TUNA LOINS

Most home cooks will never encounter a whole or headless tuna, but anglers and chefs can both benefit from learning this technique—cutting the four loins from tuna. Butchering a tuna is similar to butchering beef: Each part and muscle is treated differently in cut and how it is prepared, especially for the sushi and sashimi market.

Tuna is graded using a Japanese scale because tuna with the highest fat content will fetch the best prices in the sashimi market. Number one tuna is sashimi grade with a high fat content, good color and clarity, and highest in price; number two is similar but less fatty; number three is brown, also known as chocolate or grill-grade tuna, and will have a bitter aftertaste. Sushi-grade tuna is often served raw in sushi, sashimi, or ceviche, or seared only on the outside. When the catch of yellowfin, bigeye, or bluefin tuna arrives at the dock, a core sample is taken from behind the tail. A tuna expert will then evaluate and grade the fish before sending it to market.

Tuna are migratory fish that travel the world in dense shoals. As early as the second century B.C.E., the Greeks knew of their migratory habits, though they were still not fully understood. In Provence, until the end of the nineteenth century, the approach of shoals of tuna was heralded by lookouts blowing horns. Mediterranean tuna fishing is of great antiquity, then, as today, of considerable commercial importance. Some bluefin tuna are still caught in special tuna traps during their breeding migrations, in a capture known as *la mattanza* (or "the slaughter") in Sicily. Comparable traps were probably used in Neolithic times and were well-established by classical times. In la mattanza, a long net stretches out to sea, intercepting the migrating fish and diverting them into a series of ponds. They end up in the net where the fish are finally captured and taken from the nets with gaffs.

Over the past forty years, the adult population of Eastern Atlantic and Mediterranean bluefin tuna has declined 72 percent; 82 percent in the Western Atlantic. The International Commission for the Conservation of Atlantic Tunas (ICCAT) sets catch quotas for the fish and is supposed to curtail illegal fishing. Japan has opposed a proposal to ban the bluefin tuna trade, though some Japanese consumers have begun to worry about the future of a fish they prize. The World Wildlife Fund is trying to convince Asian buyers to shun bluefin tuna—a difficult task because savoring the best raw *maguro* (*tuna* in Japanese) is strongly embedded in its culture. Kindai tuna, which is bluefin raised from the egg stage, rather than from captured juveniles used for tuna-ranching, at Japan's Kinki University's fisheries laboratory, is now being exported to the United States for sale to high-end restaurants. Australia's Clean Seas Tuna Ltd., which has been working with the university, has produced Southern bluefin tuna from hatched eggs rather than captured juveniles and expects to start marketing the fish soon.

1 Place the tuna, in this case a 60 plus pound (27 kg) yellowfin, on a large, clean work surface with the backbone toward you and the head end facing your writing hand. Note: The small cut at the tail end is where a slice of the flesh has been removed to check the tuna's quality.

4 Now cut away the collar at the head end. Insert the knife just above the thoracic fin on the belly end and cut upward in a curve following the shape of the head.

5 Move the fish around so that its head faces your nonwriting hand and repeat the cut as in step 4.

2 Cut off the narrow tail end of the fish.

3 Using your nonwriting hand, pull up the pectoral fin and then slice it away at its base, cutting toward the tail. (The pectoral fin on tuna folds back and fits perfectly into a recess in the fish's body, streamlining it for fast swimming.)

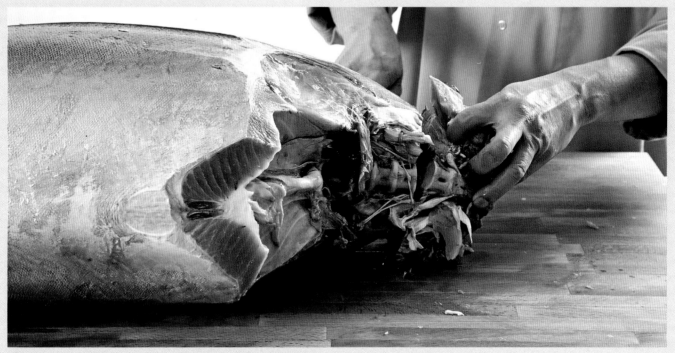

6 Grasp the head of the fish in your nonwriting hand. Cut through the fish in between the vertebrae to sever the remainder of the skull.

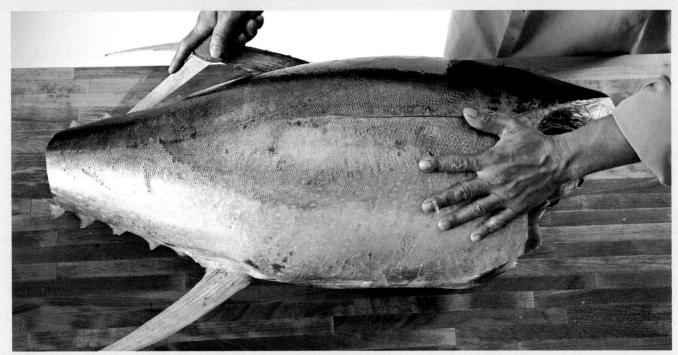

7 Now you are ready to start removing the first two loins, one below the lateral line and one above the lateral line. Insert the tip of a large fish filleting knife just in front of the triangular yellow finlets. Cut from the tail toward the head, keeping the knife as close to the bone as possible. While cutting, insert the knife as far as the center spinal bone of the fish.

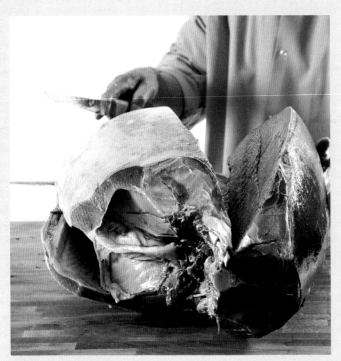

10 Lift off the top right-hand top loin, cutting to release it from the backbone as necessary.

11 Next you will remove the right-hand bottom loin, cutting from head to tail and holding the backbone in your nonwriting hand to hold the fish steady. Using the first cut as a guide, repeat the cuts, going deeper each time until you reach the backbone.

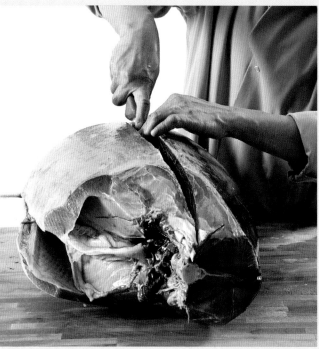

8 Turn the tuna 90 degrees so that its head is away from you. Now cut from the head toward the tail. Grabbing on to the collar end with your nonwriting hand, insert the knife into the belly, cutting from the head end toward the tail as close to the bone as possible to avoid cutting into the flesh.

9 Move the tuna so its tail end is facing you and the backbone faces your nonwriting hand. Steady the fish and cut along the side all the way through the flesh to the bone, using the first cut as a guide. Repeat, cutting from the head to the tail until you meet the cut made in step 8.

12 Remove the bottom right loin, trimming away as necessary from the backbone.

13 The very dark meat on either side of the backbone, called the blood line, is removed. Trim off any raggedy edges.

15 Starting toward the back of the top loin, insert the knife and trim off the tough white membrane.

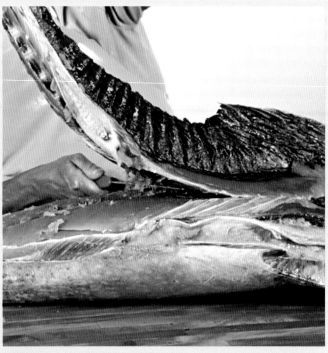

16 Next, remove the two remaining loin sections from the underside of the fish. Insert the knife just under the spine and cut toward the head while using your nonwriting hand to lift up the rear of the belly bone section.

14 Turn the tuna 90 degrees so that its head is away from you. Now cut from the head toward the tail. Grabbing on to the collar end with your nonwriting hand, insert the knife into the belly, cutting from the head end toward the tail as close to the bone as possible to avoid cutting into the flesh.

17 The remaining two loin sectins will be attached in the center. Cut down the center line all the way through the skin to separate them into two loin quarter sections.

18 Trimmed right-hand loins.

HAGEN STEHR AO (ORDER OF AUSTRALIA) HAS BEEN INVOLVED IN THE AUSTRALIAN AQUACULTURE INDUSTRY FOR MORE THAN THIRTY YEARS.

HAGEN STEHR AND JEMMA MCCOWAN:
FOUNDER AND MARKETING CONSULTANT OF CLEANSEAS

Born in Prussia, Germany, Stehr spent two years as a professional soldier in the Legion Étrangere (Foreign Legion) in North Africa before arriving in Australia, where he bought his first fishing vessel in 1961. With a background in prawn, abalone, and tuna fishing, Stehr founded the Port Lincoln, Australia-based Stehr Group in 1969, now one of South Australia's most successful fishing and aquaculture businesses. The town of Port Lincoln has been so successful with tuna fishing that it now has more millionaires per capita than any other city in Australia. Cleanseas has led the way in developing controlled aquaculture spawning and grow-out of kingfish and mulloway. Its subsidiary, Clean Seas Tuna Ltd., is developing technology to become the first company in the world to close the lifecycle of the southern bluefin tuna (SBT) so it can be bred in captivity from hatched eggs.

We also spoke with London-based marketing consultant Jemma McCowan, who has a background in international business and export marketing with the Australian Trade Commission. McCowan works with the Cleanseas network around the world to develop strong international markets for its portfolio of sustainable fish. We spoke about Cleanseas, the plight of the bluefin tuna, and what to expect in the future for tuna and other sustainable farmed fish.

Hegen Stehr holding a ranched
Southern bluefin tuna

YOUR COMPANY RAISES SUSTAINABLE FARMED FISH IN AUSTRALIA. WHERE AND HOW DOES THIS TAKE PLACE?

We operate out of a 400-hectare (4-square-km or 1.5-square-miles) site about 3 km (1.9 miles) south of Arno Bay in southern Australia, where the water is clean and cold. We use natural feeds, minimal stocking densities, and practice site fallowing to deliver fish that is totally sustainable.

WHAT KIND OF FISH SPECIES DOES CLEANSEAS RAISE?

We raise southern bluefin tuna, kingfish, and Suzuki mulloway. One species of bluefin, *Thunnus thynnus*, swims in the northern hemisphere. The second species, *T. maccoyii*, which we raise, swims in the southern oceans. Since the 1950s, the population of southern bluefin tuna has dropped more than 90 percent. While others have gotten these notoriously finicky fish to spawn and grow in ocean cages, our company has been able to coax these tuna to breed in landlocked tanks.

WHY DID YOU CHOOSE TO RAISE KINGFISH?

We raise kingfish (*Seriola lalandi*), also known as yellowtail kingfish (*hiramasa* in Japanese), because this large pelagic (ocean-going) fish presents many of the same challenges and potential solutions to breeding bluefin tuna. Kingfish can be farmed efficiently—reaching market size, 4 kg (8.8 pounds), in about eighteen months. Most of this fish goes to sushi and is well-known in Japan for this purpose. Kingfish also works well for Italian-style crudo.

HOW DO YOU GET THE FISH TO SPAWN?

We keep our wild-caught kingfish and mulloway broodstock, weighing between 25 and 30 kg (55 and 66 pounds) onshore in their own temperature and light-controlled recirculation facility. By changing temperature and adjusting light, we create a "spawning season" so that the fish will reproduce.

WHAT DO YOU FEED YOUR FISH?

We feed our fish pellets made from sustainably sourced fish meal, fish oil, wheat, lupin meal, soya, wheat gluten, vitamins, and minerals. All our feeds are NON GMO (non-genetically modified organisms).

WHAT ARE THE EATING QUALITIES OF KINGFISH?

Kingfish, a type of amberfish, also related to pompano, is renowned for its white, firm flesh. It has few bones and is high in beneficial omega-3 fatty acids. Kingfish adapts well to a large variety of cuisines from Japanese sashimi and sushi to Thai dishes. It is also excellent grilled, steamed, baked, and used in spicy salads.

YOU ALSO RAISE MULLOWAY— CAN YOU DESCRIBE IT?

Suzuki mulloway, *Argyrosomus hololepidotus*, is a member of the large croaker and drum family (croakers make a croaking sounds; drum fish make a drumming sound). Also high in beneficial omega-3s, mulloway live in South Australia and are also found in Japan where they are prized for sashimi.

WHO BUYS YOUR FISH, AND HOW DO THEY USE IT?

We export about 55 percent of our production to Europe, Asia, and North America. Our biggest market in Europe for kingfish is Italy, where a similar wild fish is as familiar as *ricciola*. Many Michelin-starred restaurants serve our fish as does Nobu at all their restaurants. One Indian restaurant in London serves kingfish with cardamom-champagne sauce. At London's famed Fat Duck, owner Heston Blumenthal buys our fish fresh then superfreezes it at −76°F (−60°C), preventing crystallization. A Japanese restaurant in Milan whose policy it is to use fish to the utmost takes the scrapings and binds them with prawns for mini-kebabs. (For our Japanese-style fillets, we leave the collar on. In fact, we have customers who only buy the collars for their rich and sweet meat.) Another French-style chef in London uses the fattier scrapings near the skin to make tartar and uses the skin to make cracklings.

HOW DO YOU LIKE TO COOK KINGFISH?

We like to cook kingfish like tuna, to no more than medium-rare to take advantage of this sashimi-grade fish and enhance its buttery moist cooked texture. Above all, don't overcook it!

A Cleanseas tuna pen in the waters of Southern Australia

MATERIALS NEEDED:

Clean cutting board

A long fish skinning knife (shown here)
or a filleting knife

Tray to hold fillets

SKINNING AND FILLETING SKATE WINGS

Here we remove the thick, tough skin from the two wavy side wings of a skate—its only edible part except for the liver—and remove the two fillets from each side: the thicker fillet on top, the thinner side underneath. Skate may also be cooked whole before removing the skin. In a small skate, the thinner fillet may be too small to be useful and is often discarded. Fan-shaped skate wings contain long, narrow bands of warm pink flesh separated by cartilage. Cooked, the ivory-white fingers of flesh are firm with moderately pronounced flavor.

Its cartilaginous flesh is extremely high in collagen and should be served piping hot, or it can feel sticky in the mouth. Poach skate wings and the resulting stock will be so stiff with gelatin that you can cut it with a knife. One persistent urban legend has cut-out circles of skate wing substituting for expensive scallops in Chinese restaurants.

Raie au beurre noir, a French bistro favorite, is prepared with black butter, which is nutty browned butter sharpened with capers and lemon. Asian cuisines rely on the strong flavors of soy, garlic, and chiles to cut the richness of skate. In their search for sustainable, reasonably priced fish, chefs are transforming this "trash fish" into treasure on a plate.

TIP

Rays and skates are cartilaginous fish, closely related to sharks. They are shaped like a kite and flattened from top to bottom (or dorsal to ventral) with eyes on top of their head and swim near the ocean floor. Rays belong to three scientific orders, while skates are all *Rajiformes*. Like other primitive fish including shark, to which they are closely related, skates taste better a few days after harvest, to allow the uric acid that builds up in their skin to dissipate. The spotted skate used here and exported from the United States to Europe is preferred to the rays, which have edible, though dark red, strong-tasting meat. The yield is 50 percent fillet from whole wings.

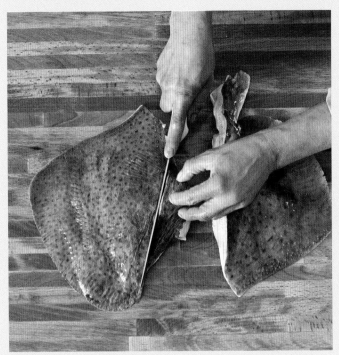

1 To peel the skate of its gritty skin, lay it on a clean cutting board, dark side up. Cut a lengthwise slice about 1 inch (2.5 cm) from the edge to expose the inner edge of the bones inside. Use a long skinning knife, if possible, to reach all the way through the fillet with a single cut.

2 Cut away the slice and discard.

3 Turn the skate wing over so its light side is up. Grasping the edge with your non-writing hand, insert the knife about 1 inch (2.5 cm) from the end and cut from the inside edge to the curved edge, cutting the flesh from the skin underneath, keeping the knife flat.

4 Skate wing fillet removed from the skin.

5 Turn the skate wing so that the flesh side is up and the flat edge faces away from your body. To remove the cartilage underneath, cut a small slit across the near side.

6 With the filleted side up, grasp the edge of the skate wing with your nonwriting hand. With your other hand, cut the fillet away from the tough skin while pulling on the edge.

9 Slice about 1 inch (2.5 cm) into the fillet, cutting toward your body. Repeat this motion until you completely free the fillet from the flat cartilage underneath.

10 Now remove the bottom, thinner fillet, inserting the knife into the far edge of the fillet just below the cartilage. Continue cutting until you have detached the thin fillet completely.

7 Continue cutting the fillet off the skin while grasping firmly on to the edge of the wing.

8 Now you have two fillets (top thick fillet and bottom thin fillet) with a thin flat cartilage separating the two fillets that must be removed. Insert the knife alongside the top fillet with the tip at the end away from your body.

11 Thick fillet, flat cartilage, and thin fillet. Repeat steps 1 through 10 with the second skate wing to get a total of four fillets, two thicker from the top and two thinner from the bottom.

CLEAN and COLD: At Samuels and Son Seafood, the cutters work at long counters with a trough of cold running water in front. This allows them to work with the knife off the edge of the table for better reach. The water is treated with harmless ozone that kills bacteria and neutralized odors helps keep everything clean as they work. The cutting room temperature of 35°F (2°C) keeps the fish at its freshest.

MATERIALS NEEDED:

Large pan or casserole to hold fillets

Sink or large bowl of cold water (for rinsing)

Clean cutting board or work surface

Chef's knife

Tray to hold cut portions

1 Look for salt-cod with ivory-colored flesh and a faint tint of green or yellow, here Canadian Atlantic salt-cod.

CHOOSING AND PREPARING SALT-COD

Cod was originally salted as a way of preserving this enormously important fish, but eventually people came to appreciate it on its own for its chewy texture and bold flavor. Decades ago, I had a hard time convincing customers to try salt-cod fritters inspired by a trip to Rio de Janeiro. With the wildfire growth of tapas bars in North America, salt-cod in fritter form and in other recipes is reaching a newly appreciative audience.

Salt-cod will keep perfectly for months if refrigerated but will give off a strong aroma if not wrapped tightly or placed in a sealed container. One pound (450 g) of boneless salt-cod yields 1½ pounds (680 g) after soaking. Boneless, skinless fillets shredded into flakes can be ready in 2 hours, while larger whole fish require up to 36 hours of soaking. Because there are so many methods of salt curing, there is no set rule for how long to soak the fish. Once the fish has soaked sufficiently, it will be plump and pliable and the soaking water will not taste unpleasantly salty. Oversoaked salt-cod will be bland and unappetizing.

The day before you plan to cook the salt-cod, rinse the cod under cold running water until you no longer feel any hard crystals of salt on the surface. Place the fish in a large bowl and cover with cold water. Leave to soak overnight, refrigerated in hot weather, at room temperature in cold weather. Change the water once or twice during the soaking period.

4 Trim the thin, bony belly covering.

2 Salt-cod fillets: salted (left) and soaked (right). Salt-cod that is overly bright white in color may have been artificially treated or may be overly salty.

3 Once the salt-cod has been soaked, trim it as shown to make individual portions of similar thickness and weight so they will cook evenly. Trim the stringy tail end.

5 Cut into individual portions.

6 Salt-cod with trimmings and five individual portions.

TIP

Never boil salt-cod. It will toughen the fish and turn it stringy. Instead, cook it gently at a bare simmer. To cook for salad or filling, drain the soaked salt-cod and place in a large pot with cold water to cover. Bring to a boil, then reduce heat and simmer for 10 minutes, or until the fish flakes easily. Drain the fish, then flake it into large chunks, making sure to remove and discard bones (if any). Some recipes such as salads may call for raw salt-cod.

The best place to look for top-quality salt-cod, which is not cheap, is at Portuguese, Spanish, and Italian markets, where the clientele is willing to pay for the best. Some retail fish markets will carry small wooden boxes of extra-salty salt-cod cut into blocks, especially in winter, and Asian markets will also sometimes sell smaller salt-cod. You can sometimes find a whole side of salt-cod, because it is so richly gelatinous that its meat is actually sticky in the mouth—perfect for any one of hundreds of Portuguese recipes for bacalao (it is said that there is at least one bacalao recipe in Portuguese cuisine for every day of the year).

MATERIALS NEEDED:

Clean cutting board or work surface

Special gutting knife or short utility knife

Bowl for salted water

Tray to store roe

EXTRACTING SHAD ROE

If your shad is pregnant with delicious fine-textured roe, it's best to remove the roe after scaling but before filleting the fish.

The best shad roe will be fully developed with yellow to orange eggs the size of small birdshot. Wash the roes carefully, removing visible blood clots, slime, and the outer, loose membrane. (The fine inner membrane keeps the eggs enclosed and should remain intact.) If purchasing the roe at a market, the roes will already be cleaned.

SHAD: EXTRACTING ROE, FILLETING, AND BONING

Here we process an American shad, *Alosa sapidissima* (the latter means "tastiest"). Shad arc basically big fat herring and are anadromous: They begin and end life in freshwater and live most of their lives swimming great distances in saltwater.

Native to the North American East Coast, shad range in their travels from the St. Johns River in Florida to the Bay of Fundy in Canada, where huge numbers of fish eventually end up. Shad are fished with hook and line, nets, and gill nets, but in the Bay of Fundy, they are captured in weirs, long badmintonlike nets set into the bay to take advantage of its huge tidal changes. The nets must be woven and built every year from spruce and fir in a method that may have come from the native Micmac Indians. As far back as the ancient Phoenicians, weirs were constructed from palm branches to catch bluefin tuna. So, the knowledge of constructing weirs was brought with colonists from Europe.

Shad have also been successfully introduced to the North American Pacific Coast. Its cousin, the European shad, *A. alosa*, has a deep blue back and silvery sides and sometimes sports a dark spot behind its gill cover. Also known as May fish, these shad fish travel up the rivers of Europe during spring to spawn.

Because of its oiliness, shad benefits from acidic ingredients such as lemon or vinegar. One of the oldest and best ways of cooking the oil-rich shad fillet is to nail it to a plank set at an angle in front of a fire burned down to coals.

3 Pull open the belly cavity. Remove the viscera, which lie over the roes, and discard.

1 Place the scaled shad with its backbone away from you and its head facing your nonwriting hand on a clean work surface. Pull back the head of the shad. Insert the gutting knife into the gill opening.

2 Slit open the belly, cutting toward the tail.

4 Open up the belly cavity and locate the roes by feeling them with your fingers. Gently pull out the pair of roes, which are enclosed in a delicate sac, separating them from the surrounding membrane.

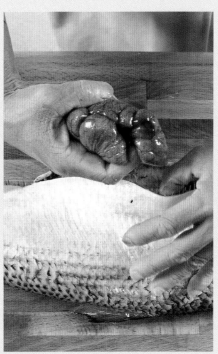

5 Keep the roes as intact as possible as you lift them from the belly.

6 Shad roe ready to cook. Soak the shad roe sets in salted ice water (¼ cup salt [72 g] dissolved in 2 quarts [1.9 liters] water) for 5 minutes before cooking.

FILLETING SHAD

MATERIALS NEEDED:

Clean cutting board

Filleting knife
(preferably a fish
filleting knife)

Tray to store fillets

1 Fresh, whole, gutted and scaled shad.

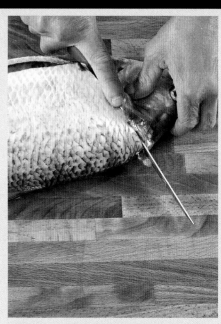

2 Place the shad with its backbone away from you and its head facing your non-writing hand. Cut away the head.

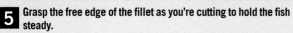

5 Grasp the free edge of the fillet as you're cutting to hold the fish steady.

6 Still holding the free edge of the fillet, sever the top fillet from the skin by cutting it away at the tail end.

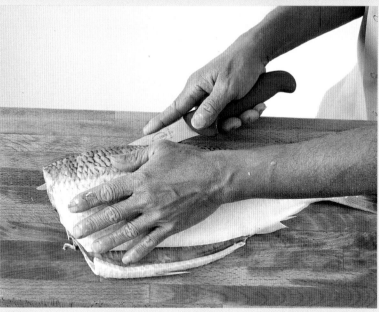

3 Turn the shad so that its backbone faces away from you and its head faces your writing hand. Insert the knife at the head end just in front of the backbone.

4 Cut along the backbone, about 1 inch (2.5 cm) into the fillet, keeping the knife into the flesh just on the top side of the backbone. Slide the knife alongside the bones and angle it toward the bones rather than toward the flesh so as not to cut into the flesh. Make a second pass: Starting from the head end again, cut all the way through the fillet to the belly.

7 Turn the fish so its backbone faces away from you and its head faces your nonwriting hand. Insert the knife above the tail and cut along the backbone, about 1 inch (2.5 cm) into the fillet, keeping the knife on top of the backbone.

8 Reverse directions and cut all the way through the fillet to the belly. Grasping the free end of the fillet, sever the fillet at the tail as in step 6.

9 Two shad fillets.

BONING THE FILLET

Shad are notoriously difficult to bone as they have a double set of intramuscular floating rib bones that lie in two rows parallel to the backbone on each side. Run your finger over the side of the shad and you can feel the tips of the bones. Shad boning is a true art—removing all 769 bones without tearing up the soft, tender flesh is not easy.

MATERIALS NEEDED:

Clean cutting board

Extra-sharp filleting knife (preferably a fish filleting knife)

Container for the bones

Tray to store fillets

1 Place the fillets with their thick (head) end facing you and perpendicular to the work surface. Using a sharp filleting knife, cut into the fillet along one side of the darker red center line starting about 4 inches (10 cm) back and cutting toward the head end.

4 The first set of small bones lies alongside about ½ inch (1 cm) toward the backbone side of the fillet. Cut into the flesh as shown.

5 Make a second cut about ½ inch (1 cm) away from the first cut toward the backbone side of the fillet as shown.

2 Make a cut parallel to the first cut on the other side of the center line to remove a long, narrow strip of flesh in the center of the fillet. Pull up the strip, trimming it away from the fish with your knife.

3 Shad fillet with center strip removed.

6 Pull open the sides of the first cut to expose the bones.

7 Make a third cut on the belly side of the center line, angling the knife as shown and without cutting all the way through the flesh. Cut about halfway down the length of the fish.

8 Pull open the sides of the second opening to expose the rib bones, cutting crosswise across the top and underneath the ribs.

9 Pull up and remove the strip of bones.

12 Pull open the third cut and cut it away from the skin at the tail end.

13 Continue cutting down the belly strip all the way to the tail.

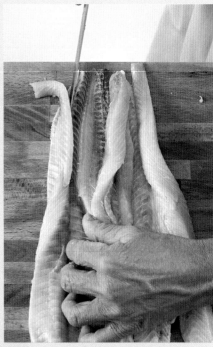

14 Pull open the sides of the belly strip and cut the tail end of the fillet meat away from the skin, leaving it attached at the other end. Cut away the third strip of bones.

10 Turn the fillet so that its tail end is toward you and continue the first cut toward the tail.

11 Continue the third cut all the way to the tail, then cut underneath the second and third cuts about one-third of the length of the fish, freeing the fillet meat from the skin. Push the strips aside to access the next set of bones. Pull open the second cut and remove the second set of bones.

The shad has inspired many a storyteller including George Washington, who wrote in his diary, "The white fish [or shad] ran plentifully at my Sein landing having catch'd abt. 300 in one Hawl." Philadelphia journalist Louis Magargee who wrote in the periodical he published, *Seen and Heard*, in 1901, "There's only one way to cook a shad. Take her squirming out of the water, run with her to an open fire, clean her quickly, nail her on a thick hickory board, stand her in front of a fire of a fierce blaze and continually baste her with the finest gilt-edge butter until she is golden brown color. That is the whole story; nothing remains but the eating." John McPhee called shad "the founding fish" in his book of the same name because of its important role in American culture.

The Micmac, a Native American tribe, told the tale that shad were originally an unhappy, discontented porcupine that asked the Great Spirit to re-create it in a different form. The Spirit obliged by turning the porcupine inside out and tossing it into the river where its bones are ready to challenge the most determined filleter.

15 Two shad fillets (right) with bones and skeleton (left and center).

JANET AMATEAU:
CHEF/OWNER OF TRADESCÀNTIA TERRACE RESTAURANT, PINEDA DE MAR (BARCELONA), SPAIN

A native New Yorker, Janet Amateau is chef/owner of Tradescàntia, an acclaimed waterfront restaurant near Barcelona, Spain, serving creative and traditional pan-Mediterranean food accompanied by live music. Amateau is a noted authority on Sephardic (Judeo-Spanish) food who has worked with the City of Barcelona, the European Days of Jewish Culture, and the Lower East Side Tenement Museum in New York, and has been featured in the *Washington Post*, the *Jewish Week*, Barcelona Televisiò, and Catalan radio. After a decade each working in international tourism and theater in New York, Amateau moved to Catalonia in 2005 and opened the restaurant. "I have loved all my careers," declares Amateau. "They've all been about sharing culture to a crazy rhythm—and a lot of improvisation."

HOW IS SEAFOOD OBTAINED FOR YOUR RESTAURANT—DIRECT FROM FISHERMEN, DELIVERED TO YOUR DOOR, FROM A MARKET?

In Catalonia, there's a regulation against restaurants buying fish right off the boat, but we buy from purveyors who buy directly and deliver to our door, or we hand select from their warehouses. We also work with smaller local markets who buy from independent fishermen or cooperatives. And all Spanish cities have municipal markets (like La Boqueria in Barcelona) with stalls that sell to the trade and the public. The quality is generally excellent—and the fish displays can be absolutely beautiful.

WHAT ARE YOUR FAVORITE SPANISH SEAFOOD SPECIES?

I would name *mejillones de roca* (wild rock mussels), *calamar* (squid), and anchovies. I am mad about Galician razor clams and Mediterranean red shrimp. There's a small sole from the south that I love, and river trout from the north.

WHAT MAKES CATALONIAN SEAFOOD UNIQUE COMPARED TO SEAFOOD IN OTHER REGIONS OF SPAIN?

Every river, sea, and ocean has a different mineral content and temperature, which affect the creatures that live in it. Catalonian seafood is varied and plentiful, but the region is especially known for anchovies and sea urchins from the Costa Brava. As far as cooking styles go, climate, geography, and local culture all play a role. We're in the Northern Mediterranean where winters are colder. The food is heartier and seafood is often prepared with thickened sauces or in stews.

WHAT WOULD BE A TYPICAL SPANISH OR CATALONIAN WAY OF PREPARING SEAFOOD?

An easy favorite is cooking *a la plancha* or *a la parilla* (on the griddle or broiled), with a sprinkling of salt and whatever the local condiment is. In Catalonia that would be *alioli* (garlic mayonnaise) or a drizzle of good olive oil. Other regions have more complicated dipping sauces that might be spicy, herbal, sour, and so on. There's *paella*, of course, and *fideuà*, which is a Catalan/Valencian paella made with toasted angel hair pasta instead of rice. Smaller, whole fish are more popular than deep-sea steaks and are typically baked or pan-fried, or started on the stove and finished in the oven with white wine, herbs, and potatoes or vegetables. Frying calamar, *bacalao* (salt cod), or *merluza* (hake) after dipping in flour is a cooking style from Andalucía that's universally popular.

ARE THERE ANY SEAFOOD SPECIALTIES THAT ARE ONLY FOUND IN SPAIN?

Spain is surrounded by water and filled with streams and rivers, and I believe it has about sixty autochthonous species. However, many species aren't consumed beyond their local region, because there just isn't enough to supply a larger population. Also, Spanish people believe that fish taste best when they're eaten at the source. Traveling to eat a certain fish is part of the fun of the gastronomic culture here. Spanish species that are widely available are *percebes* (gooseneck barnacles) and *angulas* (tiny, tiny eels from the north).

Janet Amateau conducting a cooking class in Spain

WHAT IS THE PLACE OF BACALAO (SALT-COD) IN SPANISH CUISINE?

The Portuguese built the Iberian salt-cod trade over 500 years ago, and with bacalao suddenly so plentiful and transportable, it became popular everywhere in Iberia, even inland, and was eaten by everyone. But with the onset of the Inquisition, how and when you ate bacalao could get you in serious trouble. Christians ate fish on Fridays and throughout Lent and bacalao became the emblematic Lenten fish. (Today there are Lenten bacalao festivals all over Spain.) But, it wasn't enough just to eat salt-cod. In those days Christians fried everything in pork fat, whereas Jews used only olive oil. Cod dipped in flour and fried in olive oil was a prevalent Jewish cooking style, so religious converts had to give it up or risk heresy charges. (For more on salt-cod, see "Choosing and Preparing Salt-Cod.")

I SEE THAT YOU SERVE *DAURADA LA SAL* (SEA BREAM BAKED IN SALT CRUST). IS THIS A POPULAR WAY OF PREPARING FISH IN CATALONIA?

It's popular everywhere, but it comes from the Mediterranean Coast. We also prepare sea bass this way. It's a great technique for showing off the flavor of very fresh, whole, white-flesh fish. The salt forms a crust that keeps the fish moist throughout the baking process and the skin prevents the fish from absorbing all the salt. When you break off the crust, the skin peels away with it.

DO YOU HAVE ANY "TRUCS OF THE TRADE" FOR READERS REGARDING SEAFOOD?

If you want to serve a fish *carpaccio* (thinly sliced raw fish), bone a fillet and then freeze it for twenty-four hours. First, it's an important safety issue, but it's also for convenience. It's easier to cut thin, uniform slices while the fish is still frozen, either with a sharp knife or a meat slicer.

MATERIALS NEEDED:

Large, deep container or stockpot

Coarse salt (see sidebar)

Hammer (optional, see sidebar)

Clean cutting board or work surface

Filleting knife

Work glove or rough cloth (optional)

Single-edged razor or utility knife (optional)

Needlenose pliers (not fish pliers)

Kitchen shears

Tray to store eel sections

EEL: SKINNING AND PREPARING

Eels are primitive creatures that date from early prehistoric times; it is said that the Atlantic Gulf Stream they follow on their migrations once circled the lost island of Atlantis. Because the ancient Greeks never saw a female eel with eggs, they believed eels were created by spontaneous generation. European eels travel a fantastic distance when they're ready to spawn in spring—as far as the mysterious Sargasso Sea between Bermuda and Puerto Rico. There they mix with American eels. Once the females lay their eggs, they die. The tiny elvers take three years to travel back to Europe.

In Quebec, you can find smoked eel, a centuries-old specialty. It is also popular in Northern Europe, much of which is imported from Ireland. Many Asian markets keep eel in live tanks where they are quite skilled at resisting capture in nets. Eel is on every sushi bar menu as *unagi*, its Japanese name, where it is served filleted and then broiled with a sweet soy glaze. Freshwater eels, prepared here, are long and slim with smooth, slime-coated slippery skin and spineless fins near the head. Both the European eel (*Anguilla anguilla*) and the American eel (*A. rostrata*) are anadromous, living part of their life in freshwater and part in saltwater. Most are caught in freshwater.

Eel has meat that is quite firm, high in fat, and has a distinctive, strong, full-bodied flavor. The raw flesh is pewter-gray but turns bright white when cooked, with a small, fine flake. The tough skin is not eaten. Its yield is 60 percent skinless fillets from whole eel.

TIP

Eels may be killed by grasping them (they are quite slippery, so use a work glove to get a good grip) behind the head and hitting them forcefully on the head with a hammer. Note that even after death, the eel will keep moving.

1 Place the eel in a large, deep container. Rub it with coarse salt. (The eel will keep moving, so cover it.) It should not be buried; a generous sprinkle is enough. Leave it for up to two hours to kill it and remove the slime coating. It is not necessary to scrape off the slime if you are skinning it.

2 Grasp the head end of the eel. Use a rough cloth or dip your hands in salt to keep them from slipping. Make a slit all around the "throat" of the eel, cutting through the tough skin but not the flesh. You may also use a single-edged razor blade to slit all around the eel at the "neck."

3 Cutting from the head end, slit the belly of the eel.

4 Continue cutting all the way about 1 inch (2.5 cm) past the anal opening to remove the dark red kidney.

5 Loosen the free edge of the skin with the tip of the blade. Grasp the freed skin with pliers and begin peeling the skin back toward the tail with a vigorous pull.

6 Once the skin has been removed, pull out the viscera cutting them free. Scrub the gut cavity and wash it out thoroughly to remove all traces of blood from the backbone and throat, and then rinse again.

7 Turn the eel so that its head end faces your writing hand and cut off the head. Cut off the fins using kitchen shears.

8 Cut the eel into six sections (one per portion). Alternatively, fillet the eel by slicing off the flesh on either side of the backbone. It is best to smoke the eel on the bone then fillet.

THE EXQUISITE PRESENTATION OF SUSHI MADE FROM SUPER-FROZEN, PROPERLY DEFROSTED TUNA HELPED CONVINCE ME THAT FROZEN FISH CAN BE AS GOOD, IF NOT BETTER, THAN FRESH, IF HANDLED WITH CARE AT ALL POINTS ON THE COLD-CHAIN FROM THE OCEAN TO THE TABLE.

MICHAEL McNICHOLAS:
OPERATIONS AND QUALITY CONTROL MANAGER FOR UORIKI FRESH (SUPERFROZEN FISH FROM JAPAN).

Michael McNicholas migrated from Ireland to the United States in 1984 after working in market development for the Irish government for Enterprise Ireland to spearhead its export sales program in the United States. There, he found his true passion. With Irish seafood suppliers and U.S. retailers he developed the first-ever national organic seafood program in the United States based on farmed salmon from Ireland's west coast. McNicholas next dedicated himself to bringing sustainable seafood to the U.S. retail environment and works closely with retailers, aquaculturists, and seafood processors worldwide on this complex issue. Since 2007 he has worked for Japan's premier fishmonger, Uoriki, where he manages operations and quality standards. The company's U.S. headquarters are in Secaucus, New Jersey.

YOUR COMPANY'S NAME IS UORIKI. WHAT DOES UORIKI MEAN?

Uoriki is a compound word in Japanese: *uo* means "fish" (one of many words for fish in Japanese); *riki* means "the spirit of the fish." At Uoriki, we believe in the spirit of the fish, that it's not just; a dumb object that died to provide food, but rather, it's a living creature that gave its life for our sustenance. For every creature that comes out of the ocean, we have to respect it and use it to its fullest.

Anyone who has to use all-natural products, they'll come to us. We will not handle the CO tuna, and we will not handle the CO hamachi.

"CO FISH," ESPECIALLY TUNA, HAS BEEN TREATED WITH CARBON MONOXIDE TO HELP PRESERVE ITS COLOR. WHY IS THIS CO BAD?

The simple purpose of the carbon monoxide treatment (used also for red meat) is to disguise age and quality by keeping the color bright red. Carbon monoxide has no flavor and eating treated meat alone will not make you sick. However, that supercharged color lasts up to a year, far beyond the date when steaks, ground beef, or fish are no longer safe for consumption. The use of CO is banned in the entire civilized world: It's banned in Europe, Canada, Japan, Singapore, and Taiwan. You know something is pretty horrible when it is banned in China. But yet, the United States allows it. In most of the countries, the area of law in which CO treatment is banned is consumer protection laws. It's consumer deception, that's exactly what it is.

Display of Japanese fish
at a supermarket

THE CARBON MONOXIDE ITSELF IS NOT DOING ANYTHING BAD. IS IT JUST THAT IT TAKES AWAY THE WAY YOU WOULD KNOW WHETHER THE PRODUCT IS FRESH OR NOT?

One of the ways that all of us evaluate food safety is by using a visual indicator such as color. If that's negated, you can't figure out whether something is fresh or spoiled. If you leave a CO-treated steak and a tuna out on the countertop for a week, it would stink to high heaven, but it would still look edible. The enhanced color of CO tuna also disguises grade. What might be a grade 3 fish is bumped up to a 2 plus, which is worth more money. [The lower the number, the higher the quality.] CO tuna is also known as gaspipe tuna, tailpipe tuna, clear smoked tuna and *saku* tuna, a Japanese word that means "regular shape", because it is sold already cut into thin rectangular blocks.

WHAT IS THE HISTORY OF SUPERFROZEN FISH?

Superfreezing was originally developed by the medical industry in the 1960s and 70s to keep lab samples in good condition. It is also used in blood banks and in fertility clinics to store eggs and sperm. You've heard of keeping eggs and sperm for twenty years. You've heard of test tube babies. There's only one way that could happen: superfreezing. It's as if there's been no passage of time. It sounds a little sci-fi, but that's essentially what happens. Superfrozen fish doesn't even go into rigor mortis until it has been defrosted, which may be six months after death. Normally, any living creature goes into rigor mortis four to six hours after death.

DOES THE FREEZING PROCESS KILL BACTERIA?

Freezing does not kill bacteria. You'll find live bacteria 50 million years old in the deep permafrost. At −76°F (−60°C; water freezes at 32°F [0°C]) bacteria are deactivated and become absolutely dormant. With dormant bacteria, you have no decomposition and therefore, no putrefaction.

WHAT ACTUALLY HAPPENS TO THE MOLECULES WHEN SUPERFREEZING?

If there is any continued movement whatsoever of molecules, there's deterioration. You get something down below −76°F (−60°C) and nothing moves—even water doesn't form crystals. The important thing to remember with superfreezing is that what goes in is exactly what comes out, so GIGO ... garbage in, garbage out.

WHAT IS YOUR COMPETITION IN THE TUNA MARKET?

Our biggest competitor is fresh tuna: not CO tuna, not frozen tuna. Fresh tuna feed out by the continental shelf, which is about 1,000 miles (1,610 km) from the coast. Boats need a week to get out there and a week to get back. But a week out there is just the start. The boats could be fishing for three weeks and take a week coming back. Even day-boat tuna from Hawaii is usually three to four days old. Our product is only six to eight hours old every day.

IS THERE ANY NEGATIVE REACTION IN THE MARKET TO FROZEN FISH?

There's a natural negativity to anything frozen in some markets and it's well-deserved, because it's been done terribly. But, they try this product and we teach them. I stress to customers: You're not butchering fresh tuna. What you are doing is reviving this product. If you pay as much attention to the revival as you would to butchering you're going to have a great product every single time.

MATERIALS NEEDED:

Superfrozen tuna slice, available from supermarkets including Whole Foods and Wegman's in the United States

Shallow container large enough to hold the tuna

Paper towels

Salt

Warm water

Instant-read thermometer (optional)

Plastic film

Hotel pan (optional)

REFRESHING SUPERFROZEN TUNA

As top-grade tuna becomes rarer, it's more important than ever to preserve the fish at its prime so there is no waste. Uoriki is a Japanese company that specializes in superfrozen tuna and other fish such as hamachi (yellowtail or amberjack). It relies on technology adapted from the medical field for keeping lab samples fresh. Superfrozen tuna has been available in Japan for more than 30 years and represents about 80 percent of the tuna sold there. Mainly used for high-ticket fish such as bigeye, yellowfin, and bluefin, superfreezing is relatively new to other markets, including the United States.

Superfrozen tuna is caught by longline vessels, then dressed and immediately frozen on board to –76°F (–60°C), known as the eutectic point: the temperature at which all cellular activity stops; even water crystals don't move. The fish are kept at this temperature until they're defrosted for use, basically in suspended animation. Conventional freezing methods leave pockets of heat in the water contained in cells. After defrosting, the cell walls break open and the water drains out, carrying flavor with it. Superfreezing keeps cell walls whole, so water loss is minimal, and it retards oxidation, a natural process that results in unappealing browning in tuna.

Because standard freezing methods don't prevent browning, processors infuse tuna with carbon monoxide or flavorless smoke to restore the appealing redness of fresh tuna. Also known as saku tuna (which actually refers to the rectangular shape of the pieces of tuna that are treated with carbon monoxide), this chemical process is not allowed in most of the world outside the United States.

TIP

All living creatures go through rigor mortis within four to six hours of death, a process that stiffens flesh and reduces its tenderness. Because superfrozen tuna is caught and then quickly frozen, it has not yet entered rigor mortis. Once the tuna has been defrosted, rigor mortis may cause the fish slice to shrink or change shape—proof of its freshness.

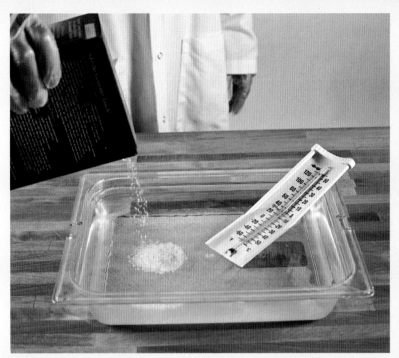

1 Defrost the tuna the night before use to obtain the fullest, richest color and flavor. Prepare a container filled with about 3 inches (7.5 cm) of warm water (between 90°F and 105°F [32°C and 40.5°C]). Add 3.5 percent of salt (any kind) into the water and mix to combine. (For 1 pint [475 ml] of water, add 1 tablespoon [18 g] of salt).

2 Rinse superfrozen tuna portion under running water to remove any dust on the outside, then place it into the saltwater bath. Allow tuna to soak for one to two minutes until it begins to regain its red color.

3 Remove tuna from water. Pat tuna dry with paper towels to remove surface water. DO NOT rub. Store two to three hours in the refrigerator allowing the tuna to defrost completely. The tuna is now ready for use.

4 Once the tuna is defrosted, remove the paper and wrap in plastic film. Do not wrap in plastic film while defrosting as it will prevent the color from developing. Refrigerate refreshed tuna up to two days. For large amounts, arrange the tuna in a hotel pan lined with paper towels, making sure they do not touch. Cover with paper towels and refrigerate.

CHRIS LEFTWICH:
CHIEF INSPECTOR TO THE WORSHIPFUL COMPANY OF FISHMONGERS', LONDON

London's Billingsgate Market is legendary because of its incredible history and the enormous variety sold there every day to meet the needs of the many ethnic groups that shop there. I interviewed Chris Leftwich, who has been employed for the past twenty-five years as the chief inspector to the Worshipful Company of Fishmongers'—an ancient City Livery Company that has had an unbroken association with the fish industry for around 1,000 years. As chief inspector, Leftwich is responsible for the quality control of all the seafood sold at the market—the premier inland wholesale fish market in the UK. In 2004, Leftwich was the main author for *Fish and Shellfish*, a comprehensive guide to seafood and the industry, written as a training tool for industry and enforcement officials. At the World Seafood Congress held in Morocco, Leftwich was elected president of the International Association of Seafood Professionals.

WHY DID YOU ESTABLISH THE SEAFOOD SCHOOL AT BILLINGSGATE MARKET?

I established the Seafood School in 2000 as a charitable company with the aim of plowing monies raised from the commercial activities for the industry and public into educating young people, especially schoolchildren, about seafood. We tend to target younger children about 8 or 9 years old as they tend to be the most receptive to changing their eating habits. If you miss them at this age it is unlikely that you recapture them until much later in life.

WHAT KIND OF CLASSES CAN PEOPLE TAKE?

The school runs a whole series of courses directed at the industry and the public accessible on our website (www.seafoodtraining.org). In our own small way we are trying to reskill the public by overcoming the myths and prejudices surrounding seafood preparation. Most people are more than happy to eat seafood when someone else does the preparation but are frightened themselves in case they mess it up. We are also putting knowledge back into the industry.

In the UK, most retail sales occur in supermarkets. However, their employees do not have the knowledge to instill confidence in the consumer. It is fine if you are already a fish consumer but the lack of knowledge and expertise is a barrier to trade for any new customers, so we train supermarket fishmongers. We've also been successful in seeing several new businesses start up as a result of our courses. Two of our trainers recently ran a short course for the inmates at UK's largest prison, Wormwood Scrubs.

CAN YOU TELL ME ABOUT BILLINGSGATE MARKET AND WHO SHOPS THERE?

Billingsgate is the largest inland fish market in the UK. We handle around 25,000 tons of seafood product per annum from all over the world. Seafood is the number one globally traded seafood commodity and we offer 140 to150 varieties of fish and shellfish daily. London is a huge cosmopolitan mix of people, many of whom are from ethnic backgrounds with a strong seafood eating tradition. Hence we strive to offer them product with which they are familiar.

WHAT IS THE HISTORY OF BILLINGSGATE MARKET AND THE WORSHIPFUL COMPANY OF FISHMONGERS?

The Worshipful Company of Fishmongers' has been associated with the market, on its present site for twenty-eight years after moving from the City of London where it operated for the best part of 1,000 years. Initially if you wanted to sell fish in the city or surrounding area you had to pay the company a levy. This was finally replaced by a Royal Charter in 1604 to oversee the quality of what was sold. I now direct a small team of quality inspectors at the market.

Christ Leftwich inspecting fish at London's Billingsgate Market

MATERIALS NEEDED:

Clean cutting board or work surface

Utility or paring knife for skinning

Tray to store fish

Fish filleting knife, preferably flexible, for filleting

DOVER SOLE: SKINNING AND FILLETING

The king of classic French and what used to be known as continental fish cuisine. Here we skin and fillet the almond-shaped Dover sole, *Solea solea*. This flatfish is full of pleasing buttery flavor and has a much firmer, almost meaty, texture than most other flatfish. You can always tell if the fish you've purchased is a true Dover sole (not a lemon sole or gray sole, which are really flounders) because its skin can be peeled off the flesh, which can't be done with any other flatfish.

Dover sole live only on the eastern side of the Atlantic Ocean. These world-famous fish get their name from the town of Dover on the English Channel, which supplied enormous numbers of sole to London's main fish market at Billingsgate (see the interview with Chris Leftwich to learn more about Billingsgate Market). Dover sole range from the Mediterranean to the North Sea and are usually found in shallow waters. In Italy delicate-tasting smaller sole from the shallower though saltier Adriatic are preferred and are a favorite with children either steamed or dusted with flour and pan-fried in olive oil.

Sole are right-eyed flatfish that spend most of their lives lying flat on the sea bottom. Restaurant chefs love sole because they yield thin, firm fillets that hold their shape in cooking. To keep them at their juiciest, sole are best cooked on the bone and may be filleted tableside at high-end restaurants.

The top side of a Dover sole is brown with darker blotches and a black spot on each pectoral fin. The thin, silvery membrane underneath the skin after the fish has been peeled is known as the *shine* in the UK.

The average weight of a Dover sole is about 1 pound (450 gm). Do not confuse the unrelated flatfish, *Microstomus pacificus*, also known as Dover sole, that is found along the Pacific coast of North America, with European Dover sole. Its yield is 40 percent.

TIP

To prepare Dover sole for grilling, slice through the center or lateral line of the fish from head to tail, then cut away from the bone on either side to open up the fish, as if you were filleting it but without cutting all the way, to create a "collar." Repeat on the other side. Snip the bone at the head and tail with scissors but don't remove. After the fish is cooked, you will be able to easily lift away the bone.

SKINNING DOVER SOLE

1 Note the almond shape and rounded head of the true Dover sole.

2 Place the Dover sole on a clean cutting board dark side up and its tail facing your nonwriting hand. Using a sharp knife, scrape up a little of the skin from the base of the tail end.

3 Use your nonwriting hand to grab on to the base of the fish, using a kitchen towel, if desired, to get a better grip. Holding the fish down with the other hand, grasp the end of the skin and peel off from the tail toward the head.

4 The skin should detach in a single piece.

5 Turn the fish over so that its light side is up. Holding the fish down with the other hand, grasp the end of the skin and peel off from the tail toward the head.

FILLETING DOVER SOLE AND PREPARING FOR GRILLING

If you're planning to roast or broil a Dover sole, peel off only the top skin, which is thicker, leaving the tender white skin on the underside, which adds flavor and rich body when the fish is cooked.

1 Place the skinned Dover sole on a clean work surface with its tail facing your nonwriting hand and its light side up. Insert the tip of a knife into the belly just in back of the head. Slide the knife toward the tail, cutting underneath the viscera and through to the backbone.

3 Continue cutting, keeping the knife close to the bones, while grasping the free end of the fillet with your other hand.

2 Use your nonwriting hand to lift up the free end of the fillet. Insert your knife at the head end of the fillet and cut across the backbone and across the width of the fish.

4 Turn the fish over so that its dark side is up and its head is facing your nonwriting hand and grasp the head. Repeat steps 2 and 3 on the darker side.

5 Two fillets of Dover sole.

ZARELA MARTINEZ, WHO WAS BORN AND RAISED IN
SONORA, MEXICO, BEGAN COOKING PROFESSIONALLY
DURING THE LATE 1970S IN EL PASO, TEXAS, WHERE SHE
CAUGHT THE ATTENTION OF SEVERAL INFLUENTIAL CHEFS
FOR HER AUTHENTIC MEXICAN REGIONAL COOKING, ESPE-
CIALLY THE SEAFOOD-BASED CUISINE OF VERACRUZ.

ZARELA MARTINEZ:
OWNER OF ZARELA RESTAURANT, NEW YORK CITY, AND COOKBOOK AUTHOR

With the encouragement of chef Paul Prud-homme and *New York Times* food writer Craig Claiborne, she made some notable guest-chef appearances. In 1983 Martinez moved to New York as menu designer and then executive chef for Cafe Marimba before opening Zarela in 1987. Martinez introduced food lovers to the Mediterranean- and African-accented regional cooking of Veracruz with her PBS series *Zarela! La Cocina Veracruzana*. She is the author of its companion cookbook, *Zarela's Veracruz* (Houghton Mifflin Harcourt, 2001), *Food and Life of Oaxaca: Traditional Recipes from Mexico's Heart* (Wiley, 1997), and *Food from My Heart: Cuisines of Mexico Remembered and Reimagined* (Macmillan, 1995).

WHAT IS UNIQUE TO THE CUISINE OF VERACRUZ?

Veracruz, which is on the Gulf Coast, has a lot of African influence. This region was the first place where slaves were actually liberated, in 1628. Its food has a lot of African influence, which is also seen in the herb and spice mixtures in many dishes. There's more of an African mix in that part of the country than many Mexicans even recognize.

The food of Veracruz also has a very Mediterranean style. What is wonderful is you don't need a lot of specialized ingredients other than *hoja* (or *hierba*) *santa* [bunches of herbs called sautéing herbs, which usually includes cilantro, chives, and mint, are sold in markets]. In Veracruz, the cooking is based more on herbs than it is on spices.

Veracruz has a unique cuisine in the mountains, which run along 400 miles of the state. The coast also has a unique cuisine. Plus, Veracruz borders on seven different states, which means that there are influences of seven regional cuisines. It's a very complex state and very exciting. In my opinion, this is the best food in all of Mexico: It's varied and accessible.

WHAT ARE SOME OF YOUR SEAFOOD COOKERY SECRETS?

I always simmer seafood in stock, either lobster stock or fish stock. And that accentuates the flavor a lot. Straining the stock and reusing it a few times makes a very enriched stock, such as in a *bouillabaisse* with its layers of flavor. That's exactly my style of cooking: layers of flavors.

WHAT ARE SOME VERACRUZAN SEAFOOD SPECIALTIES?

There is a fisherman's *torta de mariscos*, which is filled with seafood. They also make an omelet filling of *camarones*. Then there's *huachinango a la Veracruzana* [red snapper stewed Veracruz style with capers, olive oil, tomatoes, parsley, and green olives], which is one of the most popular dishes in my restaurant. The tomatoes and chiles are from the New World. This dish is a perfect fusion of cuisines, though it is so often redone and overdone—and not in a good way.

In Veracruz there's all the seafood you can get! The shrimp are fantastic—we call them camarones; we call the larger shrimp *gambas*. There is also lots of crab and lots of warm-water oysters, so most of the appetizers at Zarela's are related to seafood.

WHAT IS THE SEAFOOD CUISINE ON THE WEST COAST OF MEXICO?

The West Coast is known for its shrimp dishes. In the homes, when they serve a fish they serve a big fish first, and then if people are still hungry they serve a medium-sized fish, and then if people are still hungry they'll serve a small fish. The use of dried shrimp is in everything—tamales, salsas. It's a very arid land and very hot, so they don't have a lot of vegetables there.

ON THE PACIFIC COAST, IS RAW FISH PART OF THE CUISINE?

We don't have much raw seafood in Mexico, though the ceviches are starting to catch on. *Bacalao* (salt-cod) is used practically everywhere in Mexico. It is *the* Christmas dish.

WHAT IS UNIQUE ABOUT THE SEAFOOD OF MEXICO'S CARIBBEAN COAST IN YUCATÁN AND QUINTANA ROO?

There is a lot of raw seafood eaten there, and they also eat a lot of conch. The cuisine has an Arab influence because there was some immigration to that part of Mexico. That region was very isolated from the rest of the country for a long time, so it has more ties to the Caribbean islands. It was also where prisoners were sent.

In Yucatán, they have dishes such as a *tabbouli* made with sour orange and habanero. The trademark spice paste might have come to the region with the Spanish, because we didn't have spices other than native allspice at the time. The spice mixtures may have originated in Lebanese or Moorish regions.

The native Mayan details are cooking in a pit (*pibil*), cooking with a particular type of green beans, and using achiote [or annatto, *Bixa orellana*, very hard dark red seeds that impart a deep red-orange color to food].

WHAT KIND OF CHANGES HAVE YOU SEEN IN MEXICO'S SEAFOOD CULTURE?

I'm very much into conservation. A friend of mine took me out to sea in a skiff traveling from one uninhabited island on Mexico's Pacific Coast to the other where we saw stacks of shells. If you dig down inside the stack, you can find out what seafood species used to be common in that region. Today, because of the chicken farmers, a whole local fishery has been destroyed. There are no more sardines because the chicken farmers take the sardines and feed them to the chickens so they grow faster

and can get to market one week earlier. In the food chain that one thing has already been destroyed. Mexicans are getting better at conservation, but it's really hard to talk to people about it.

HOW IMPORTANT IS SUSTAINABILITY IN YOUR PART OF THE WORLD?

I think poor people who live in villages aren't naturally wasteful. I asked a man in a little village that I wrote about quite a lot, "Does the rise in prices affect you?" He said, "It doesn't affect me. We eat the same thing all the time: beans, chili, potato, tortilla, salsa. That's it." There's a particular tradition among the Mexican Indians where they use the plant at every single stage of development: roots, tendrils, leaves, fruit, and the seed. You get an incredible range of different nutrients from each plant at its different times of development.

ARE THERE ANY PARTICULAR SPECIES OF SEAFOOD THAT YOU SAY WOULD BE USED MOST IN MEXICO?

I use a lot of warm-water oysters. My mother used to eat a hundred of those oysters raw, just off the shell. In Veracruz, they do an amazing *ostiones a la pimienta*, oysters cooked in a sauce with black pepper, jalapeños, and onion. They are to die for!

MATERIALS NEEDED:

Clean cutting board or work surface

Utility knife

Chef's knife

Tray for fish

CLEANING SQUID

Here we'll clean and cut up fresh young squid, one of the first techniques I learned from the hands of a master, Marcella Hazan. I used to buy 50-pound (22.7 kg) boxes of squid and clean them one by one. The bodies were destined to be dredged in seasoned flour and deep-fried, but I was after the delicate, anise-flavored ink, which I used to make my own black pasta and black risotto. Today, chefs can order fresh, cleaned squid and containers of squid ink from wholesalers. Though many restaurant menus have moved beyond fried squid, these cephalopods are nearly always called by their Italian name, *calamari*.

Squid are cephalopods with a fleshy cigar-shaped soft body containing a single thin, transparent, flat, pen-shaped vestigial "bone." Fins on either side keep the squid balanced, and it has ten arms, two of which are long tentacles that they use to grab their prey. Squid shoot their dark ink at their enemies to protect themselves, though cuttlefish, or ink squid, contain much larger quantities of the ink. They swim in schools and will frequently follow the schools of fish on which they feed—in turn tuna follow the squid and eat them. Squid inhabit all the oceans of the world.

The long-finned or winter squid, *Loligo pealei*, is preferred in the kitchen because its meat is finer in texture and more tender than the less expensive, short-finned or summer squid, *Illex illecebrosus*. The Pacific squid, *L. opalescens*, is a North American West Coast favorite and is in season beginning October or November when they school close to shore for spawning. Giant Pacific Humbolt squid, *Dosidicus gigas*, which can reach 7 feet (2.1 m) long and weigh up to 110 pounds (50 kg), are quite aggressive. Known in Mexico as *diablos rojos*, or red devils, it is believed that these squid hunt in packs and reports have them attacking divers with their razor-sharp beaks.

In Japan, squid cut in a special way is eaten raw in sushi; in China and Korea dried flattened squid and cuttlefish are a popular street snack. Some Korean markets have a special machine that cuts slits into the squid so it looks like a set of jalousie blinds. *Calamares en su tinta* (squid cooked in its own ink) is a classic Spanish preparation, while deep-fried squid rings, invariably called by their Italian name, calamari, are ubiquitous on Italian-American menus. Asian markets are a good place to look for fresh squid, which should be shiny, resilient, and sweet smelling. All parts of squid and cuttlefish are edible except for the eyes, mouth area, inner organs, and the clear hard "bone."

The elusive giant squid, first photographed by Japanese researchers in 2004, can be as much as 43 feet (13.1 m) long for the larger females and is one of the world's largest living creatures.

Because their meat is made up almost entirely of albumin protein (like egg whites), squid and other cephalopods work best cooked very quickly (grilling or deep-frying) or very slowly (braising). Large squid are often stuffed before slow cooking. Raw cephalopods, including squid, octopus, and cuttlefish, absorb liquid quickly, so marinate no more than 24 hours or the flesh will turn mushy.

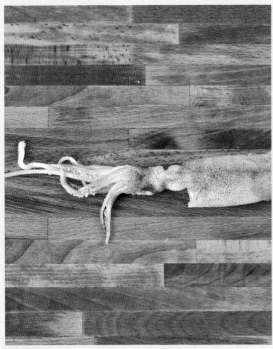

1 Lay the squid on a clean worktable with its head toward your nonwriting hand.

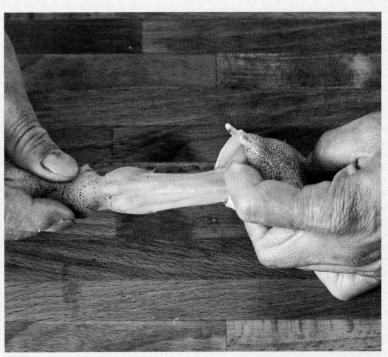

2 Grasping the body in one hand and the head in the other, gently pull apart until the head with viscera detaches from the body. The small ink sac will be covered with a silvery membrane. If the ink sac is broken, it can stain. The ink is useful in cooking. Ink squid (cuttlefish) will have much larger ink sacs and darker ink.

3 If it doesn't come out with the viscera, pull out the thin clear bone from inside the body of the squid.

4 Press your finger the length of the body. Pregnant squid will contain a soft white substance that should be squeezed out. Rinse out the inside of the body.

5 Separate the purplish-pink spotted skin from the body, removing the wings at the same time.

6 Remove the skin. (Some prefer to leave the skin on for cooking; it is gelatinous and adds body to sauces.)

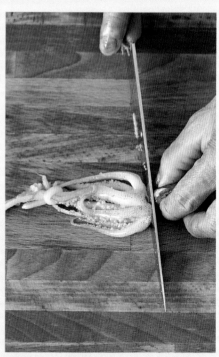

7 Lay the head down on the worktable with the tentacles long and straight. Cut away the tentacles just above the squid's eyes. Trim the two long tentacles to match the others, if desired.

8 Hold the tentacles in one hand with the tentacles pointed down. Peel the tentacles back to make an open flowerlike shape to reveal the inedible beak. Squeeze up from the bottom in the center so the beak pops up. Twist it off and discard.

9 Cleaned squid and tentacles.

CUTTING THE SQUID

Option 1. Cut the mantle into rings using a chef's knife. These are often deep-fried.

Option 2a. Cut the mantle into strips with a chef's knife.

Option 2b. Open up the squid body. Cut lengthwise strips. These will curl up into ringlets when cooked.

Squid separated into edible and inedible body parts. Left to right: inedible clear bone, fins (edible though tougher than the body), mantle, beak, viscera head with tentacles.

MATERIALS NEEDED:

Large pot or sink

Cold saltwater

Cornmeal (optional)

Clam knife

Protective glove (optional but recommended)

Crushed ice

Platter for serving

PURGING AND OPENING HARDSHELL CLAMS

Like scallops and mussels, clams are bivalve mollusks. They live buried in mud or sand with two shells (or valves) that are hinged together by a tough elastic ligament. They use their muscular foot to propel themselves forward.

Here we will purge clams of the sand that they naturally contain and open them to serve on the half shell. Whether you like your clams raw on the half shell, baked casino style with seasoned bread crumbs, or with linguine in white wine sauce, clams have a strong salty taste of the sea and are relatively tough. Because you're working with live, raw shellfish, it's especially important to work very clean. Anyone with a compromised immune system should not eat raw clams. For safety, only prepare or eat clams that are tightly shut or that close firmly when tapped (if the clams are icy cold, they may have to warm up before closing when tapped). The shells should be moist and the clams should have a sweet, clean, ocean smell. Discard any clams with broken shells or those that gape open. You should hear a solid sound, like billiard balls knocking together, when you gently tap two clams together. A hollow sound is a sign of a weak clam that is either dead or close to dying, which should be discarded. Sometimes you may open a clam and find that it is a "mudder"—dead and filled with mud inside—these should also be discarded.

To begin, place the clams in a sink or large pot of cold saltwater (use ½ cup [150 g] salt to 1 gallon [3.8 liters] of water). Add ½ cup (70 g) cornmeal to help whiten the meat if desired. Leave the clams to purge for 30 minutes to 1 hour. Scoop the clams from the water, leaving the sand and grit behind. Have ready a clam opening knife (see "A Few Good Tools"). It is highly recommended that you wear a protective glove on your nonwriting hand.

1 Wearing a protective glove, grasp a single clam in your nonwriting palm with the hinge facing your thumb joint and the point curving away from your wrist. Insert the knife between the two shells at the back of the clam, slightly toward the inside curve. You may need to use a good deal of steady force to push the knife into the clam. Continue pushing the knife into the clam, most of the way around the shell opening.

4 Once that muscle has been severed you will be able to open the clam. Run the knife back through the curve while twisting it to force the clam open.

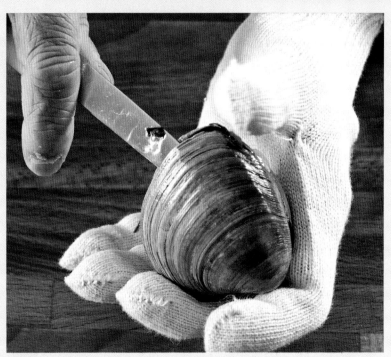

2 Switch the position of the clam, with its back edge facing up, moving the knife so that the tip is now moving inward, rather than against the edge, at the inside curve of the opening. Go back to the inside curve.

3 Run the knife all along the back of the shell, pointing it upward so as not to cut into the clam meat. When you reach the largest end of the curve, you will be severing the adductor muscle that the clam uses to keep its shell closed.

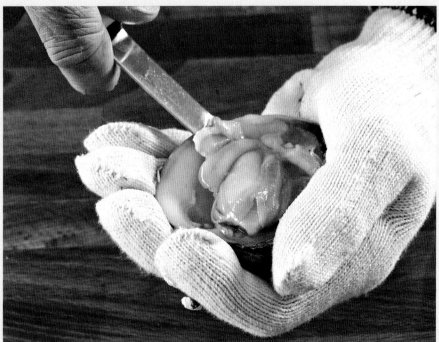

5 Pull open the top shell of the clam. Twist off the top shell leaving the clam meat nestled in the bottom shell.

6 Starting on the inside curve of the clam, insert the knife under the clam meat, and following the outer curve, scrape to sever the clam from the shell, cutting through the other side of the adductor muscle at the rear. Continue cutting all the way around until the clam meat is completely free from its shell. Note: The goal here is to free the clam from its shell without cutting into the meat. The clam is now ready for use, served on a platter of crushed ice.

MATERIALS NEEDED:

Clean cutting board

Protective glove (optional)

Clam knife or filleting or utility knife

Container to store scallops

CLEANING LIVE SEA SCALLOPS AND BAY SCALLOPS

Scallops are easy to cook, striking on the plate, versatile, and work well with all sorts of flavors and cooking methods, from pan-searing, to grilling, to baking and sautéing. Bay scallop meat may be as small as a pencil eraser; a sea scallop may be as large as a powder puff, with the larger ones stronger in flavor and smaller ones sweeter and more delicate.

Most, but not all, scallop species have ridged shells that radiate out and may be colored everything from creamy-white to pink and even orange, as in the bay scallops we are preparing here.

Like clams and mussels, scallops are bivalve mollusks. Unlike the others, scallops move quickly across the ocean floor by opening and closing the shells, pushing out water to propel themselves, developing an extra-large large adductor muscle. A live scallop shell should close tightly when tapped. Near the hinge, where the two valves (shells) meet, the sides flare out, forming "wings." In the U.S. market, typically the plump, meaty marshmallow-shaped adductor muscle, or "nut," is eaten, partly because almost all scallops are shucked on board and everything but the nut is discarded. In Europe, scallops often come to market whole and the firm, fat, curved neon-orange coral is a delicacy.

Because scallops cannot hold their shells closed, once they are out of the water, they lose moisture quickly and die. Fresh live scallops such as the ones here are kept partially closed with flexible rubber bands. These have smooth white shells, though most scallops have the classic scalloped-shape shell. Scallops from a fast-water current are best, because the water brings them an abundance of food so they will be firm and flavorful with little, if any, grit.

A clam knife works best for cleaning scallops. It is highly recommended that you wear a protective glove on your nonwriting hand when shucking scallops and other bivalves.

CLEANING LIVE SEA SCALLOPS

1 Preferably wearing a protective glove, grasp the sea scallop in your hand with its curved shell down in your palm and the hinge facing your wrist. Once the rubber band is removed, the scallop will naturally gape open.

2 Insert the knife into the scallop facing upward and scrape away at the top of the shell in order to free the scallop meat from the shell. Scrape as closely as possible to the shell to minimize loss of the precious edible adductor muscle. Work all the way around the scallop from the far edge above your thumb to the hinge.

3 Pull open the top shell. Use your knife to scrape away the thin circular membrane on the top that covers the white scallop meat and roe.

4 Membrane released from the top shell covering the scallop meat.

5 Use the tip of the knife to pull off the circular membrane, cutting it away from the matching bottom circular membrane at the hinge end of the shell.

6 Now use the tip of the knife to detach the circular membrane from the bottom of the shell. Cut off the membrane all the way around the reddish-orange roe and the white scallop meat, leaving the scallop and roe attached to the bottom shell.

7 Cut away and discard all the dark viscera near the hinge end of the shell.

8 Opposite the roe, you will see a small extra muscle attached to the main muscle called the "sweet meat." While quite flavorful this part is also tough. Pull or cut it off and save if desired to add flavor to seafood stock.

9 Slide the knife under the white adductor muscle to sever it from the shell. The intestinal vein runs all around the muscle like a belt.

CLEANING BAY SCALLOPS

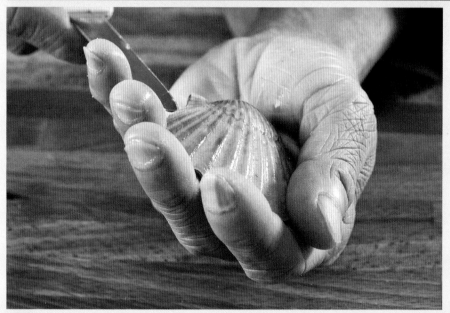

1 Hold the scallop in the palm of your nonwriting hand with the hinges facing toward your wrist. Insert the tip of the clam knife just past the small wing that sticks out on the side of the hinge. With your knife pointed up, cut toward the inside top of the shell to sever the adductor muscle from the top of the shell.

2 Open up the shell, showing the circular membrane that covers it on both sides.

3 Use the tip of your knife to pull off and remove the circular membrane, along with any dark viscera toward the hinge of the shell.

4 The clean bay scallop, ready to be cooked in its shell.

IN THE MID-1980S MANY VIETNAMESE IMMIGRANTS WITH FISHING EXPERIENCE FROM THEIR NATIVE COUNTRY FOUND A SECOND HOME ALONG THE GULF OF MEXICO COAST IN LOUISIANA, MISSISSIPPI, ALABAMA, AND FLORIDA. LIKE SANDY NGUYEN'S FATHER, THEY OFTEN TURNED TO FISHING AND SHRIMPING AS WAYS TO SUPPORT THEIR FAMILIES WITH LONG HOURS, HARD WORK, AND MUCH STRUGGLE.

SANDY NGUYEN:
FOUNDER OF COASTAL COMMUNITIES CONSULTING

The first wave of Vietnamese war refugees worked in seafood processing plants or as struggling shrimpers, sometimes going to sea in very small boats. Most came from Phuoc Tinh, the Vietnamese coastal region where they also worked as shrimpers and fishermen. Whole families would sometimes spend months at sea and life was very difficult. Extended families would save enough for each nuclear family to buy their own boat. With the second wave of Vietnamese refugees beginning around 1978, the community grew much larger and they started to be able to afford bigger boats.

Unfortunately, there were bitter feelings between the U.S. and Vietnamese fishermen over shared fishing grounds. Non-Vietnamese docks refused to allow Vietnamese-American boats to dock. Wholesalers refused to buy their shrimp and any that were willing to buy from them were ostracized. After some violent incidents, Vietnamese-American and white shrimpers began to work together to fight against low shrimp prices (about half of former prices), rising costs, environmental regulations, shrinking stocks, and inexpensive imported shrimp. Since that time, many Vietnamese-American shrimp fishermen have prospered. Second-generation Vietnamese-Americans such as Sandy Nguyen, who speak English and Vietnamese fluently have been able to help their fellow shrimp fishermen wade through government forms and regulations. I spoke with Nguyen about the life of a Vietnamese shrimp fishermen, the challenges that they face, and how the nonprofit organization that she founded is helping Gulf fishermen.

HOW DID YOUR FAMILY GET STARTED IN THE SHRIMPING INDUSTRY ON THE GULF COAST?

As new immigrants, we were looking for warm weather and water, because fishing was the only thing that we knew from our homeland in Vietnam, where my dad was a commercial fisherman. He was part of the first generation to come to the United States after the Vietnam War. Shrimp fishing was an easy business to get into and didn't require a degree. At first, Dad worked as a deck hand, saving and saving to buy a small boat, then saving again until he could afford to buy a bigger boat. In the United States, if you didn't go through school, Dad would put you on the boat. Mom learned how to shuck oysters and worked two shifts a day to send us to college. After college, I worked as a shrimp fisherman, but with my schooling and experience, I could help other fishermen with licenses, grants, and permits. My family raised me in the house as a traditional Vietnamese girl so I'm bilingual, which is a big help in the industry.

WHAT KIND OF VESSELS DO YOU USE TO CATCH SHRIMP?

There are four different kinds of vessels fishing for shrimp in the Gulf of Mexico. The smaller vessels use skimmer nets and go out and back the same day. A slightly bigger vessel will go out for three to four days beyond the 3-mile (4.8-km) state limit. The next size vessel, like my husband's trawl boat, goes out for ten to twelve days. All these smaller vessels pack their shrimp on ice and bring them to port fresh. It's the captain's decision whether to bring the shrimp in whole or remove the heads first, depending on the price difference at the dock. Most Vietnamese fishermen have the four-to-five day trip boat. The very expensive factory vessels go out beyond the federal 200-mile (322-km) limit for thirty to thirty-five days. These boats freeze their catch right onboard individually and pack them in huge sacks, thousands at a time. Each kind of vessel uses a different kind of net for the shrimp.

CAN YOU DESCRIBE A TYPICAL DAY OF A SHRIMP FISHERMAN?

The daily routine is simple though it's hard work. On the trip to the first fishing site, the deck hands will sleep, because once the vessel starts dropping its nets, the work goes on twenty-four hours a day. The nets go down every four to six hours. Two good deck hands can sort a netful of shrimp in about an hour. Once the net has been emptied, it goes right back down. In between, the deck hands will sleep, eat, shower, and get ready for the nets to be pulled up. On my husband's boat, he and a deck hand sort the shrimp, throwing back the bycatch that they can't use and bringing back fish to eat at home.

WHAT KIND OF SHRIMP DO YOU HARVEST FROM THE GULF OF MEXICO?

We get pink (*Penaeus duorarum*), white (*P. seriferus*), and brown (*P. aztecus*) shrimp, which are all priced according to size. (Whites are the mildest with sweet firm meat, pinks are the largest, usually sold whole because of their large heads, while brown shrimp have a pronounced iodine flavor.) We sell our iced shrimp at the dock right onto the conveyor belt where they are taken for processing and freezing. Everything comes down to us getting a higher price at the dock for the shrimp that we bring to market.

ARE ANY OF THE SHRIMP SOLD FRESH?

A lot of small-scale skippers or their wives will bring fresh shrimp to farmers markets where they get a better price than at the dock. Some people will drive a truck full of fresh shrimp up north to sell. They can make killer money that way. People with bigger boats don't have the capacity to go into that large ice hold to bring up a couple of hundred pounds of shrimp to sell.

DO VIETNAMESE IN THE GULF OF MEXICO FISH FOR ANYTHING ELSE BESIDES SHRIMP?

We do have about thirty Vietnamese-owned long-line vessels that fish for pelagic (open ocean) species like albacore and big eye tuna, though that fishery is heavily regulated by the government. Shark is a big-time business because of Asian demand for shark fins, but there is now a moratorium on it and the fines are pretty hefty. (The sharks also get into the shrimp nets and foul them.)

WHAT KIND OF WORK DO YOU DO NOW?

I help fishermen with the complex application process to get state funding, which has been especially important since Hurricane Katrina [in 2005], through a 501(c)(3) nonprofit organization that I founded: Coastal Communities Consulting (CCC). So far, I've helped more than eighty fishermen, which I can do well because my folks went through the same thing and I grew up in the business. I work with both Vietnamese and non-Vietnamese fishermen, trying to get them to understand each other. They may argue, but when anyone is in distress, it doesn't matter if they're Asian or white; they'll help each other.

DEHEADING, SHELLING, AND DEVEINING FRESH SHRIMP (OR PRAWNS) TWO WAYS

Fresh live Santa Barbara spot shrimp: They get their name from the four bright white spots on their bodies located on both sides of the first and fifth shell segments.

The roe of Santa Barbara spot shrimp is delicious and makes a beautiful garnish.

The U.S. market seems to have an endless appetite for shrimp. In what may be an apocryphal story, visitors to the desert city of Las Vegas, full of casino hotels, eat upwards of 60,000 pounds (27,000 kg) a day! Supermarket shrimp have almost invariably been frozen and defrosted. The longer they sit on ice, the more juices they lose. For shrimp, wild is definitely better, and those that come from farms have little flavor and unappealing mushy texture. Black tiger shrimp from Asia are cheap and abundant, which is the best thing you can say about them.

Shrimp are extremely perishable, so fresh shrimp are normally found near the coast or at top restaurants that pay for air freight.

There are a vast number of shrimp species worldwide, divided into three basic categories. Cold-water or northern shrimp are usually quite small and used for inexpensive shrimp salads. Their intestinal vein is so small that it isn't removed. Warm-water, southern, or tropical shrimp, are most of the larger shrimp served in restaurants for the ubiquitous shrimp cocktail. Warm-water shrimp from the Gulf states (Florida, Alabama, Mississippi, Louisiana, and Texas) represent the overwhelming majority of domestic shrimp harvested in the United States. Freshwater shrimp, also known as prawns, such as the Hawaiian blue prawn, comprise the third category.

Santa Barbara spot shrimp, *Pandalus platyceros*, also called California or Santa Barbara spot prawn, are called *tarabaebi* in Japanese and found on many a sushi presentation. Spot shrimp have pink to red shells with sweet, firm flesh. They live in rocky areas from Alaska to the Mexican border. If you find spot shrimp, look for the delicious roe under their belly shells—it's a beautiful garnish for ceviche or seafood salads.

In the U.K., the terms *prawn* and *scampi* are often used interchangeably. Prawns are usually freshwater shrimp or large saltwater shrimp while scampi is a restaurant term that erroneously describes shrimp sautéed in butter with garlic and white wine. (Scampi are actually lobsterettes or Dublin bay prawns, *Nephrops norvegicus*.) These thin lobsterlike creatures are pale pink to rose-orange with claws, unlike shrimp, which have no claws. Recently, it has become more common to call freshwater shrimp prawns and saltwater prawns shrimp making it all even more confusing.

TIP

Don't discard shrimp shells, which are full of flavor. True shrimp lovers will suck the delicious juices from the heads. Cover shrimp shells with cold water, add herbs, pickling spices, garlic, lemon and/or white wine, and a bit of onion, celery, carrot, and fennel, or even crab boil. Bring to boil, skim as necessary, and simmer about 30 minutes, or until the vegetables are soft. Strain and use for a cooking liquid for poaching shrimp, for fish or seafood chowders, and for seafood stews. Cool and then freeze for up to three months.

DEVEINING SHRIMP (OR PRAWNS) FROM UNDERNEATH

You can also remove the intestinal vein from shrimp from the underside. This technique is used for sushi shrimp because it makes a prettier presentation with all the pink of the skin showing.

TIP

Do not overcook shrimp, as they quickly become rubbery and mealy. I put them into a pot of boiling liquid, stir them well and turn off the heat, letting them set in the hot water until their flesh just becomes opaque and the tails begin to curl. Shrimp will lose about half their weight in shelling and cooking.

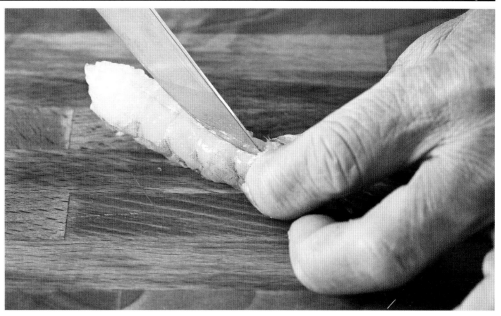

1 Position the shrimp flat with its back on the table. Grasping the tail end of the shrimp in your nonwriting hand, insert the knife at the tail end and begin to cut, butterflying the shrimp and without cutting all the way through. Continue to cut, opening up the shrimp, exposing the intestinal vein.

2 Grasp the end of the intestinal vein and gently pull it out.

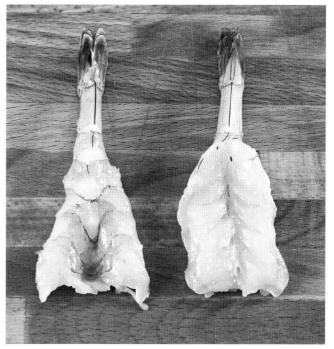

3 Butterflied shrimp from the back (left); butterflied shrimp from the front (right).

DEVEINING SHRIMP FROM THE TOP

1 Head-on wild brown shrimp from the Gulf of Mexico.

2 Hold a shrimp in your nonwriting hand at the fattest part of the body, and hold the head section in your writing hand.

5 For very large shrimp, sometimes the center sharp pointy rear fin shell is removed. To do so, grasp the pointy tip with your writing hand and gently push it from side to side to break the shell free.

6 Gently pull off the shell, leaving on the last section of shell and the tail shell to help keep the shrimp juicier when it is cooked and to provide a handle. You may remove the shell completely if desired.

7 The tail shell removed. This part will have the deepest pink color when the shrimp is cooked.

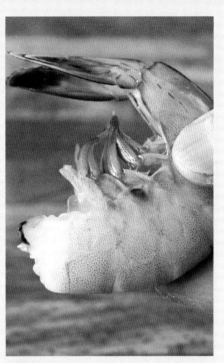

3 Gently twisting, pull the head away from the tail. Note: The small tube connecting the head section and the tail section is the intestinal vein. If this tube is clear and empty it does not need to be removed. The head contains the tasty fat and a lot of flavor. Many people cook shrimp whole and suck out the juices from the head.

4 Hold the tail section of the shell in your nonwriting hand. Grasping the shrimp on its last shell section, which is left on, pull off the front shell sections including the long feelers.

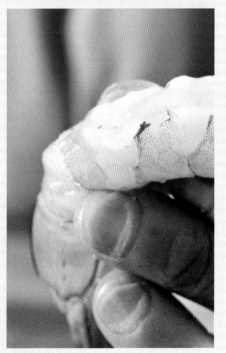

8 Next we will be removing the intestinal vein from the back. Insert the blade of the knife into the center of the back of the shrimp, about ¼ inch (6 mm) deep. Cut from the head end as far back as the last tail section, exposing the intestinal vein. Remove it using the tip of the knife to pick it up.

9 Cleaned shrimp ready to cook.

TIP

Instead of cleaning the tougher head of the octopus of its beak and eyes, you may elect to cut off the head, discard it, and use only the tentacles.

1 Place the octopus on the worktable with the head facing your nonwriting hand. The viscera is located in the round pouch just in back of the eyes.

CLEANING OCTOPUS

Octopuses are cephalopods like squid, but they have only eight tentacles to the squid's ten. Octopuses are found in warm and temperate ocean waters throughout the world where they feed on crustaceans and mollusks, which gives them their delicious flavor.

The ancestors of the mysterious octopus lived at least 20 million years ago. These intelligent creatures are built for defense—they can shoot ink and change their skin color to confuse their enemies. A large octopus can be scary to handle at first, but we're here to take the mystery away.

The octopus most commonly found in the market weighs about 3 three pounds (1.4 kg) before cleaning, although most octopus is sold cleaned. Raw octopus is purplish or brownish-gray in color. Like squid, all parts of the octopus can be eaten except for the eyes, mouth area, and inner organs. The tentacles are the most tender portion. Some octopuses at the market have been pre-tenderized by tossing them in a special machine that knocks them about. The skin around the head is quite tough and is best discarded.

Choose a fresh, glossy octopus that quickly changes color when poked. If you touch the suction cups with your fingers, they should grip firmly.

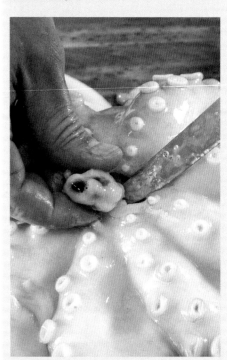

4 Turn the octopus inside out, so that the center of the tentacles is exposed. Find the dark hard beak. Using your knife, cut all around the hard dark beak and the white membrane covering it.

2 Turn the pouch inside out and pull away the viscera (including the plasticlike bony sticks and the stomach sac). Discard it all.

3 Push the pouch to the side and use a knife to cut away the viscera.

5 The octopus is now ready to be cut up or cooked whole. The eyes may be removed if desired.

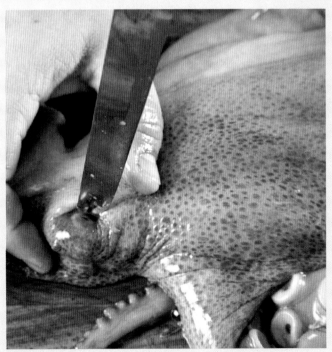

6 To remove the eyeballs, press the octopus against the cutting board so that the eyes are facing your writing hand, and the skin is taut. Cut a slit near each eye, then press firmly on the octopus. The eyes will protrude, making it easy to cut all around with your knife, or with kitchen shears to remove them. Rinse the octopus well before cooking.

MATERIALS NEEDED:

Clean cutting board

Kosher salt

Clean toothbrush (an old one will do)

Container of cold water

Clam knife

Kitchen knife

Tray to hold abalone

CLEANING AND TRIMMING LIVE ABALONE

Abalone is both a jewel and a delectable meat. Curved ear-shaped abalone shells sport a row of rounded openings that get gradually larger at the shell's outer edge. Inside, the shell has a thick inner layer of nacre, or mother-of-pearl, which in many species, is highly iridescent, and is used in jewelry making and other decorative arts. Gone are the days when we could buy fresh wild abalone, an expensive, but delicious, slow-growing single-shelled sea snail. The large, strong foot, or its adductor muscle, sticks to any surface it's attached to, and it is the edible portion of the animal (just as it is in scallops; see "Cleaning Live Sea Scallops and Bay Scallops").

Wild abalones are found in the coastal waters of every continent except the Western Atlantic Coast in South America, the Caribbean, and the United States. Abalones are most prolific in the cold waters of the southern hemisphere in New Zealand, South Africa, and Australia, and in the Western Pacific in North America and Japan. Today, China and Taiwan raise more than 90 percent of the world's farmed abalones in saltwater pens or suspended cages. They are also raised in Japan. It takes three to four years for an abalone to reach market size of four to six whole abalone per pound (nine to thirteen per kilo), so their high price is understandable. Because it's much smaller and younger than the wild, farmed abalones, it is also more tender, though it still benefits from a little pounding. The meat is light beige when raw and creamy-white when cooked, with a delectably rich, sweet flavor.

Fresh abalone is highly perishable. When live, the abalone should be lively and stick hard to the tank. As with octopus, the foot muscle should respond to the touch. If the abalone doesn't move or its flesh stays indented where it has been touched, the abalone is either dead or close to death and should be discarded (not before removing and cleaning the beautiful iridescent shell). Abalone should always be cooked the same day it is purchased.

1 Farm-raised abalone ready for cleaning.

2 Sprinkle the dark edges surrounding the abalone with kosher salt to help clean by abrasion.

3 Grasp the abalone in its shell in your nonwriting hand. Using a clean toothbrush, rub gently back and forth over the black portion. As you rub, the black coating will come off. Continue brushing the black portion, including the curly edges. Note that for large wild abalone the black portion is quite tough and will be trimmed.

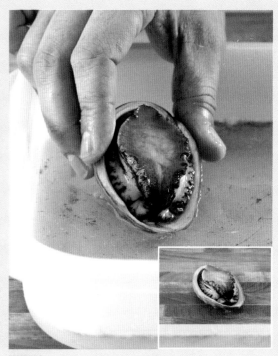

4 Rinse the abalone in a container of cold water, swishing around to clean. Washed abalone ready for trimming.

TRIMMING THE ABALONE

1 Insert a clam knife or a narrow icing spatula between the shell and the meat of the abalone. Continue cutting underneath the abalone meat all the way around, until you have freed it from its shell around the sides.

2 Insert the clam knife into the bottom center of the abalone, with the knife as close as possible to the shell. Cut the meat away from the shell.

5 Cleaned abalone turned upside down and ready for slicing. The other side of the abalone has a rim of ruffled black tisue, which was scrubbed in step 3 of Cleaning Abalone. The remainder is edible. For larger abalone, cut away the dark ruffled edge.

6 Cut thin even slices horizontally through the abalone.

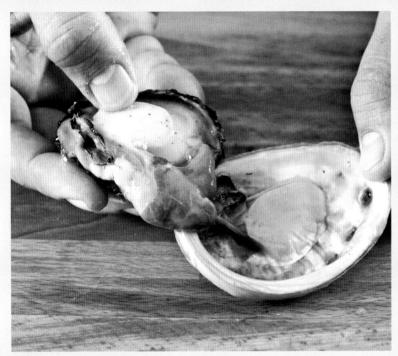

3 Lift the abalone from the shell.

4 Switching to a kitchen knife, cut away the hard viscera at the pointy end of the abalone meat, keeping the dark green cone-shaped liver whole, if desired.

7 Abalone slices. Trim off the tough outside edge of each slice. Note that the dark green abalone liver is a sushi delicacy.

MATERIALS NEEDED:

Clean towel

Clean work surface

Protective glove

Kitchen shears

Kitchen spoon, silicone spatula, or icing spatula

Tweezers (optional)

Salted water

Bowl for water

1 Preferably wearing a protective glove, place the sea urchins on a cutting board. Insert heavy kitchen shears into the hole on the domed top of the sea urchin.

CLEANING LIVE SEA URCHIN

Here we learn to remove the five paired sections of delicious roe that line the insides of the shell from a live purple sea urchin (their shells are covered in long porcupinelike spines). There are about 500 species of sea urchins worldwide; the most valuable are the red, green, and purple. They are considered a great delicacy in many parts of the world, including France (*oursin*), Italy (*riccio di mare* or *echino*), and Japan (*uni*, a term also used to refer to the roe), for their refreshingly clean iodine taste. French-Canadian fur trappers brought their taste for sea urchin from France to North America where they found Pacific Northwest Indian eating them with gusto.

The French developed a special tool, a coupe-oursin, for cutting open the shell, which is similar to cutting off the top of a soft-boiled egg.

Sea urchins are echinoderms (like the sea cucumber) that often attach themselves to rocks or to floats. Those gathered by divers from deeper waters are prized most. Fresh sea urchin roe has a mild, nutlike flavor that reminds some people of crayfish. The roe may be eaten as is or passed through a sieve to remove the outer membrane, cooked or raw. Under the spines, a thin hard convoluted round shell contains the star-shaped, yellow-orange curved mass that is the edible portion and is either the gonads of the male or the eggs of the female.

Ready-to-eat roe (available in Asian markets) should taste sweet and have a smooth, rich, buttery texture. Choose sweet-smelling live sea urchins with the inner membrane that encloses the roe completely intact, and prepare them the day they're purchased or harvested. Roe at the market has been soaked in a mixture of alum and a salt solution, similar to the mix used to keep kosher pickles firm, to keep its firm texture.

4 Carefully run a kitchen tablespoon, silicone spatula, or thin-bladed icing spatula under the roe, along the inside of the shell. The roe is incredibly fragile; try to keep it whole.

2 Cut around the top of the shell toward the outer edge in a circle shape, exposing the flesh, making an opening 2 to 3 inches (5 to 7.5 cm) in diameter. Pour away the liquid and the dark viscera from inside the shell.

3 Sea urchin with top removed. Inside are five pairs of roe that run from top to bottom on the inside of the shell: These comprise the edible portion.

5 Use your fingers or tweezers to remove any remaining viscera attached to the roe.

6 Rinse the roe in cold, salted water (about 1 tablespoon [18 g] of kosher salt to 1 pint [473 ml] of water). Store the roe in a bowl of clean salted water to firm it and flavor it. Drain well and eat raw with a squeeze of lemon or cook briefly before eating.

MIKE DASSATT HAS BEEN LOBSTERING SINCE 1983; SHEILAH COMES FROM A FISHING FAMILY THAT GOES BACK FOR FIVE GENERATIONS. HER FAMILY ALSO BUILDS DOWNEAST TRADITIONAL LOBSTER BOATS, WHICH IS HOW THE COUPLE MET.

SHEILA AND MIKE DASSATT:
CO-FOUNDERS OF THE DOWNEAST LOBSTERMEN'S ASSOCIATION, BELFAST, MAINE

The Dassatt's lobstering boat,
F/V (fishing vessel) Sarah Louise

In 2006, Sheila became executive director and Mike secretary/treasurer of the Downeast Lobstermen's Association, created in 1991 "by the fishermen and for the fishermen" to speak to the government about fishing issues, laws, supporting the fishery, and maintaining their traditional way of life in Maine. The two work very hard for the well-being of fishermen and their families because they share the same lifestyle. Mike is the captain of their fishing vessel and Sheila works right along with him.

Sheila's father, a retired fisherman and tugboat captain, taught them the trade from his boat, *F/V Red Baron*. Now, 86 years "young," he still has his lobster license and goes out with them on the *F/V Sarah Louise* every chance that he can. We spoke about the life of the lobsterman—and woman— and the life of the amazing Maine lobster, whose health and abundance they depend on for their living.

SHEILA, HOW DID YOU GET INTO LOBSTERING?

I am at least a fifth-generation lobsterman, so I came naturally by it. I was born on the isle on the eastern part of the coast. Mike's family came from Sicily, Italy's fishing center. When they got to Ellis Island, they changed their name from Dassatti to Dassatt.

CAN YOU EXPLAIN THE PROCESS OF LOBSTERING?

Before we go out lobstering, we set up the bait bags ahead of time. These are 10-inch (25.5-cm) mesh bags full of herring. Today, we buy herring but years ago we'd catch our own with gill-nets. For years, we'd go to a local sardine factory to pick up their trimmings, but it closed this year.

We get up at daybreak and head out in our lobster boat, generally staying within the 3-mile (4.8-km) state limit [from shore]. We set out a string of about 300 lobster traps, ten to twelve pots in a string, spaced about 100 feet (30.5 m) apart. Our pots are attached to hot-pink buoy markers so we and others will recognize them. We tend our traps every three days. We'll haul in a string, empty the pots of lobsters, and start sorting. I lay the lobsters on a table with dividers to keep them from fighting with each other.

Once we bring the lobsters onboard, we first sort them for sex, checking to make sure no females have eggs under their belly or a tail with a V-notch, both of which we put back in the water. (Lobstermen cut a notch in the tail of a mature female to let others know to leave them behind.) Next, we measure the lobsters using a bronze metal gauge. The sternman gets to do all the work, including banding the lobsters with thick rubber bands to hold their claws closed. Then we slide the trap down the rail to put the string overboard and move on to the next.

MIKE, WHAT IS THE DESIGN OF THE TRAPS?

The traps have a kitchen and a parlor. The lobsters first venture into the kitchen. From there, our bait bags lure them into the parlor where escape vents surrounded by biodegradable steel rings allow undersized lobsters to escape but trap the full-sized lobsters.

CAN YOU EXPLAIN MOLTING (LOBSTERS SHEDDING THEIR SHELLS SO THEY CAN GROW)?

As they mature, lobsters molt less often. Full-grown lobsters will molt about once a year. Their seasonal shedding is brought on by warm water and weather change. In summer, the lobsters come closer to shore to shed in warmer water, about 58°F to 62°F (14.5°C to 17°C). Lobsters live in deeper water in water at about 55°F (13°C). Once they molt, they are quite vulnerable, so the lobsters will move out of rocky areas and bury themselves in mud for protection while their shells firm up (four to five days). August and September is soft-shell lobster season. I try to avoid taking soft shells though they do taste the best. The first thing a lobster will eat after molting is crab shells to firm its new shell.

MIKE, CAN YOU TELL ME ABOUT THE COLOR OF LOBSTER?

The shell color a lobster has when it's alive develops according to the water in which they live and what they eat. Each lobster has its own shell pattern and colors: a combination of aqua blue, orange, yellow, dark green, red, and royal blue. I caught one lobster that resembled a leopard: It had an orange-yellow shell covered with black spots in the shape of a rainbow.

MIKE, I'VE HEARD ABOUT THE LEGENDARY BLUE LOBSTERS— HAVE YOU EVER CAUGHT ONE?

Yes, blue lobsters are really rare but I've caught one or two. Their color is beautiful, aqua to royal blue. Blue lobsters prefer colder water.

SHEILA, HOW DO YOU KILL AND COOK YOUR LOBSTERS?

We don't boil them; we steam them, which is not the fastest way but makes for a juicier lobster. We put enough water in the pot so about one-third of the body will be submerged and bring the water to the boil. We add the live lobsters, cover the pot, and cook them in their own steaming juices. A lobster doesn't have a nervous system that feels pain like humans. In summer we take a stove on our boat and steam soft-shelled lobsters in saltwater. The softer shells are easy to crack and the meat is sweeter.

MIKE, DO YOU HAVE A PREFERENCE FOR MALE AND FEMALE LOBSTERS?

Taste-wise, the female is meatier and juicier but how I do things, I don't want to deplete our stocks so I put the females back, especially the larger ones: The bigger the lobster, the more eggs it produces.

MIKE, DO YOU SELL YOUR LOBSTERS DIRECT?

In summertime, we sell to "dock and dine" restaurants on the Maine coast. After Labor Day we don't have the local trade so our lobsters are shipped to Canada for processing. Unfortunately, the timing of when we have lobsters and when we can sell them at top price for the fresh market just don't match. Sheila and I figured out that we could run lobsters to New Orleans and Houston by truck and it would only add a small amount per-pound to the price, so that's a possibility.

MIKE, WHAT IS LOBSTER SEASON IN MAINE?

We don't all fish at the same time. In Western Maine down to New Hampshire, they'll start in June. Downeast, we start in July as the lobsters move east up the coast. There's a limited supply at first so the price is higher. By the time the lobsters get to the other end of the coast, the market is saturated and starting to overflow, so the price goes down.

CHOOSING THE SIZE AND SEX OF A LOB

Select a lively lobster that wiggles its claws, trying its best to grab on to you. Its tail should spring right back when straightened, and the shell should be hard and thick. Lobsters should be alive and lively immediately prior to cooking. A lobster can live out of the water for two to three days if kept in a moist and cool place because it can extract the oxygen from the air, but its gills must be kept moist. Hard-shelled lobsters live longer than those with soft shells.

LOBSTER: SELECTING AND PREPARING

KILLING A LOBSTER

Here we dispatch a lobster quickly and humanely.

MATERIALS NEEDED:

Clean cutting board

Chef's knife

Half-sheet pan or serving tray

The American lobster, *Homarus americanus*, is a slow-growing crustacean found in the waters of North American Atlantic coast. The European lobster, *H. gammarus*, is a close cousin to its American cousin, but tends to be smaller with thinner-shelled claws. Although many other crustaceans are also known by the same name, only true lobsters have large claws.

The most common size of lobster at the market is 1¼ pounds (575 g), the minimum size, or 1½ pounds (675 g), which is preferable because the larger the lobster, the higher the proportion of meat it will contain. However, larger lobsters not only weigh more but also cost more per pound. The exception to this is if you buy a large lobster that is a "cull," which is a lobster with one or both claws missing, or with the tiny replacement claws regenerated when a claw is torn off. Culls must be cooked the same day they're purchased, as they will not live long.

Just after a lobster molts, its shell will be relatively soft and its meat will be juicy but sparse. Although many chefs, including me, prefer female lobsters for their delicious and colorful roe (known as the coral), environmentally speaking, it's important to leave mature females in the water to reproduce. A lobster will yield about 25 percent meat.

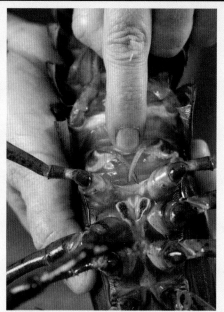

1 The lobsters shown here weigh 1½ pounds (675 g). Female lobsters have shorter, fatter tails; males have longer, narrower tails (shown).

2 Turn the lobster over. The first set of feelers underneath the tail, just past the thorax (or main body), is soft and flexible on a female (shown here).

3 On a male (shown here), the first set of feelers underneath the tail just past the thorax (or main body), is hard and shell-like.

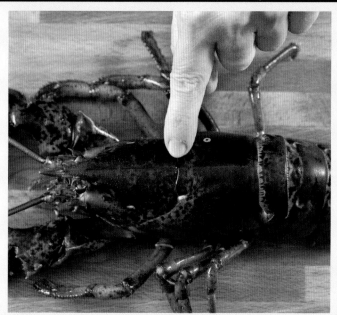

1 To kill a live lobster, place it first in the freezer for 20 minutes to slow its metabolism and dull its senses. Grip the lobster on the back of its thorax, or main body shell, just behind the front of the head as at the point shown. Note that a lobster cannot reach behind its head with its claws, though they are usually bound with heavy rubber bands for extra security.

2 Locate the place where the head shell connects to the main thorax, or body shell. Plunge the point of a sharp and heavy chef's knife between the shell sections. This will kill it instantly, although it may continue to move briefly. Place a small cutting board on top of a washable tray, such as a half-sheet pan or a serving tray, to catch its precious juices.

CUTTING UP RAW LOBSTER

MATERIALS NEEDED:

Clean cutting board

Chef's knife

Bowl for lobster pieces

Hammer or meat mallet

Container for lobster meat

Container for lobster shells

Container for coral (if using mature female lobster)

1 To remove the meat from the tail, twist off the tail at its base.

4 Remove and discard the stomach sac—now cut in two—from inside both sides of the head just in back of the eyes.

5 If desired, cut the tail into three or four sections (one section per portion).

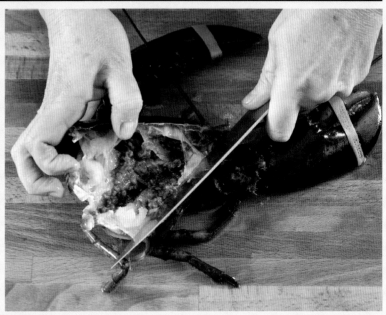

2 To extract more flavor from the head section, split it in two, exposing the tomalley, the roe, if any, and the stomach sac.

3 Some people prefer to remove the greenish, curled-up tomalley (the liver) from inside the body (shown here). Others add tomalley to a sauce to give it extra flavor. On a mature female lobster, the roe will lie inside the body and inside the shell and will be dark green in color. Remove the roe, keeping it in one piece if possible.

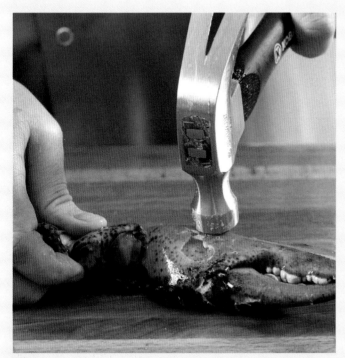

6 Using a hammer or meat pounder, gently crack the claws at their thickest part. Note that the crusher claw has a much thicker shell than the pincer claw.

7 Crack the "knuckles" above the claws to make it easier to extract the meat once it's cooked. Unlike a shrimp, it is necessary to cook a lobster before removing its meat.

COOKING AND REMOVING THE MEAT FROM A LOBSTER

Here we remove the meat from a cooked lobster. At home, most lobsters are cooked in a pot of boiling water, while in restaurants, lobsters are often killed with a quick stab behind the head, and then immediately cut up.

To cook lobster, bring a large pot of salted water to boil or set up a steamer in a large pot containing enough water to cover the bottom of the steamer. Add the live lobster to the pot and cover. On a very large lobster, break the crusher claw shell before cooking.

MATERIALS NEEDED:

Large cooking pot

Steamer basket (optional)

Salt

Clean cutting board

Kitchen shears

Lobster pick to remove small bits of meat (optional)

Bowl for the lobster meat

Bowl for the juices

Bowl for the shells

1 Cook until the lobster is bright red. The tomalley should be green and firm, the roe bright red, and the meat creamy-white, elastic, and opaque. The tail shell should be curled up, but not too tightly, an indication that the lobster has been overcooked.

4 There is very little on a lobster that goes to waste. The body portion will impart a great deal of flavor to a broth. Only the stomach sac, which lies under the top shell and just in back of the eyes, must be removed. Here we're pulling up the shell to expose the stomach and other organs.

5 Remove the stomach sac.

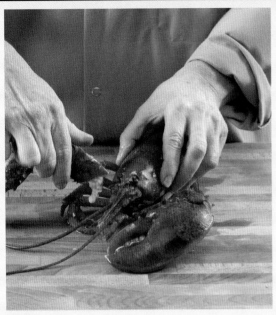

2 To clean a cooked lobster, first pull off the claws, twisting them off where they meet the body.

3 Twist off, rather than cut off, the tail, which will separate from the body with some of the meat from inside the body, leaving the tail meat intact. Notice the white and clear juices from the lobster on the worktable. All of this flavorful liquid can be scooped up and added to the pot for making sauces and soups.

6 If the lobster weighs at least 1½ pounds (675 g), pull off the feelers, which also contain thin meat. To remove the meat from them, break or cut off the larger end and push the meat out as though squeezing toothpaste from a tube.

7 Use kitchen shears to snip up the center of the tail's underside.

8 Break the back of the shell by bending it in the opposite direction.

9 The lobster tail meat will release from the shell. Gently pull out the tail meat, wiggling it at the tail end so it will release from the five fan-shaped tail shells.

12 Pull out the lobster claw meat, keeping it in one piece if possible.

13 Whole lobster claw meat from the pincer claw.

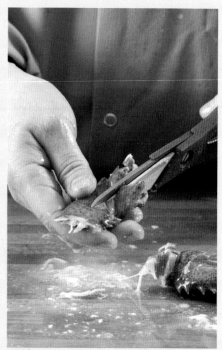

14 Twist off the "knuckles" from the claws. Use kitchen shears to cut open the knuckle sections.

10 To remove the claw meat, tap the thickest part of the shell with a hammer or a meat pounder, cracking the shell. Sometimes the "thumb" portion will pull out. Ideally, it will be attached to the rest of the claw.

11 Jiggle the "thumb" portion of the shell at its base to release the lobster meat inside. Gently pull out the meat from inside the shell.

15 Pull open across the sides and remove the meat.

16 Lobster meat, shell, and juices from a single lobster.

FRANZ SYDOW:
VENEZUELAN RESTAURATEUR AND FOUNDER OF ARUBA GASTRONOMIC SOCIETY

While at an intensive three-day course on beef from stockyard to table, I met Franz Sydow, a fellow student, and then food and beverage manager at the Wyndham Hotel, Aruba (now the Westin). A native of Caracas, Venezuela, Sydow created Sake House, a Japanese restaurant that expanded to three locations including Aruba where he moved to open the restaurant. In Aruba, he also opened Cuba's Cookin' and Pasion Restaurant before taking a position at the hotel. Sydow is a Master Sommelier and one of the founders of the Aruba Gastronomic Association. When Sydow told me that his dream was to write a cookbook about the food of Aruba, I immediately responded that I'd love to work with him. After making eight wonderful trips to Aruba (and a short visit to Venezuela), I co-authored the full-color cookbook *Aruba Tastes & Tales* with him. Since then, Sydow moved back to Venezuela to become general manager of the Hotel Jirahara, Barquisimeto.

Strawberry grouper from the Caribbean, a favorite fish for grilling

WHAT ARE SOME VENEZUELAN SEAFOOD SPECIALTIES?

It depends on the region of the country. On the islands of Margarita and Los Roques, it is the Caribbean lobster. In the north it's the trademark Caribbean fish such as red snapper, mahimahi, wahoo, and kingfish. In the west, it's blue crab, sea bass, and *curvina* (or corvina).

HOW IS BUYING SEAFOOD DONE IN VENEZUELA—DIRECT FROM FISHERMEN, THROUGH SUPPLIERS, OPEN MARKETS?

It also depends on the region of the country. On the coast and island are seafood open markets and fishermen. In the south it is done through seafood distributors.

DO YOU HAVE ANY "TRUCS OF THE TRADE" FOR READERS—ANY TRICKS THAT THEY CAN USE IN PREPARING FISH AND SEAFOOD?

Very simple: We prepare fish dishes with lots of cumin and spices. Also, we use quite a bit of green lime and garlic to season our fish.

WHAT KINDS OF TRENDS DO YOU SEE IN SEAFOOD IN VENEZUELA—ARE PEOPLE EATING MORE, ARE THEY EATING DIFFERENT ITEMS?

The trends are very Peruvian: dishes such as ceviche and *tiraditos*. People here are eating quite a bit more seafood as it is perceived as healthy.

ARE THERE ANY SEAFOOD SPECIES THAT ARE NO LONGER AVAILABLE IN VENEZUELA?

Spiny lobster is becoming quite rare. Oysters, mussels, and even shrimp are very hard to find.

CAN YOU TELL ME ABOUT SEAFOOD IN VENEZUELA'S CULTURE?

Seafood is eaten in all regions across the country, but choices are very regional. All towns that are on or near the coast are seafood friendly. Preparation in restaurants have a Spanish influence: paella and lots of garlic. Also, we love to eat the entire fish, including the very nutritious eyes! Venezuelan native recipes are very simple.

IS CEVICHE A GROWING TREND IN VENEZUELA?

Yes it is, but we use the traditional recipe with green lime as in Mexico. People are using all sorts of things to marinate ceviche but particularly orange and grapefruit juices.

WHAT IS YOUR FAVORITE SEAFOOD? WHAT IS YOUR CHEF'S FAVORITE SEAFOOD?

I love oysters, served just with green lime! Our chef loves spiny Caribbean lobster with the very simple *salsa rosada*, a version of Thousand Island dressing with ketchup and mayo.

MATERIALS NEEDED:

Clean work surface

Kitchen shears

Lobster or nut pick or cocktail fork

Hammer or meat pounder

Container for crab

1 Cook the crab as for lobster (see "Cooking and Removing the Meat from a Lobster," step 1). Place the cooked crab on the worktable with its face away from you.

CLEANING DUNGENESS CRABS

Here we clean a live Dungeness crab, *Cancer magister*, though the same method will work for other large crab species such as the European common crab, *C. pagurus*. Dungeness crabs, which get their name from a small fishing village on the state of Washington's Olympic Peninsula, are found on the Pacific Coast from Alaska to Santa Barbara, California. Peak crab season is late spring and early summer in Alaska and British Columbia, with Washington and Oregon next followed by California.

Live Dungeness crabs are reddish-brown with short, thick legs, and weigh an average of 2 pounds (900 g) though they may reach 4 pounds (1.8 kg). When cooked, the shell turns light orange and the cooked meat will be opaque ivory-white with reddish-brown edges. The dense, sweet meat is flavorful and semi-nutty; the leg meat is firmer though stringier than the rich body meat.

Piles of Dungeness crabs catch the eye at every fishmonger's stall at Seattle's Pike Place Market, usually displayed with the underside facing up.

Dungeness crabs are at their buttery, juicy best cooked and cleaned within hours of harvest. Dungeness is usually eaten right out of the shell, though San Francisco hotels have made crab Louis salad famous.

TIP

For a more humane way to handle a live Dungeness crab, place it in the freezer for 20 minutes to slow its metabolism and dull its senses. Then proceed to cook the crab or kill it. Drive an awl or a heavy-duty skewer into the underside of the crab through the shell and flesh and out its mouth at the front of the crab to kill it instantly.

Do not eat the organs of a crab, including the creamy-textured "butter" (the pancreas) of Dungeness crab as they may contain a natural toxin, also occasionally found in live scallops, that can result in paralytic shellfish poisoning (PSP). Where or when the toxin is found is unpredictable, but high levels have been found in the crab population, especially those from Alaska.

2 Twist off the large claws at their base.

3 Lift off the top shell of the crab from the back. Pull it off, revealing the interior of the crab body.

4 Find the inedible, feathery "dead man's fingers," actually the lungs of the crab. Pull off and discard them, reserving the body.

5 Rinse the body in cold water to wash away the viscera.

6 Twist off the remaining claws.

8 The backfin meat, which is contained in shell-enclosed sections, is exposed.

9 Crack the claws by tapping lightly with a hammer or meat pounder. (This step can also be done at the table by your guests.)

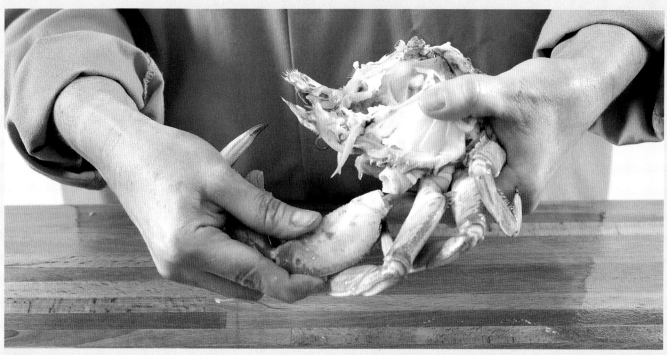

7 Grasp the main body of the crab with two hands and firmly snap in two (or use kitchen shears to cleanly cut it in half).

10 Twist the claw "thumb" at its base to release it from the shell.

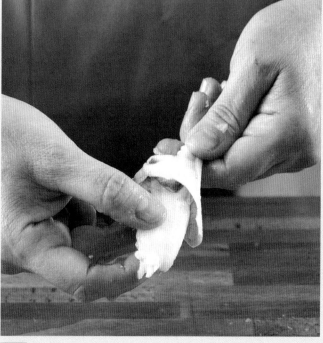

11 Gently pull out the claw meat, keeping it whole if possible. When serving whole Dungeness crab, use a nut pick or cocktail fork to remove the "knuckle" meat or suck it out as if using a straw.

MATERIALS NEEDED:

Clean cutting board

Kitchen shears

Container for cleaned crab

1 A soft-shell crab should feel like parchment paper. The shells harden quickly within a day or two after molting. Test by pressing into the top shell. The shell should indent easily.

CLEANING SOFT-SHELL BLUE CRABS

During its two- to three-year life span, a blue crab outgrows and sheds its shell about twenty times. Once the crab has molted, the new shell takes about four days to harden—leaving a small window of time in which the crabs may be eaten whole. Just after shedding, the blue crab's shell is soft enough to eat. Watermen (Chesapeake Bay crab fishermen) harvest soft-shell crabs as *peelers* (getting ready to shed), *rank peelers* (ready to shed), and *busters* (in the process of shedding).

Because they deteriorate so quickly, soft-shell crabs should be alive until they're prepared for the pan, although some processors clean and pack them to be cooked within a day or two at most. Soft shells are almost entirely and deliciously edible with a salty, sweet taste redolent of the shallow marshes where they live. Once you've eaten your first soft-shell crab sautéed in butter or battered and deep-fried, you'll crave that crab forever. Hard shell crabs, usually sold in bushel baskets, must also be alive before cooking though they are hardier than soft shells.

4 Lift up the shell from the other side, and pull out the gills.

2 To clean a soft-shell crab, place it on the work surface with its claws away from you and its top shell up.

3 Lift up the top shell from the side to locate and remove the "dead man's fingers," the spongy feathery gills.

5 Crab with all the gills removed.

6 Turn the crab over. Find the point of the apron and lift it up.

7 Pull the apron back and twist it off where it meets the body.

8 Using kitchen shears slice off the front of the crab (or its face) just in back of the eyes. Squeeze out the soft viscera from under the top shell.

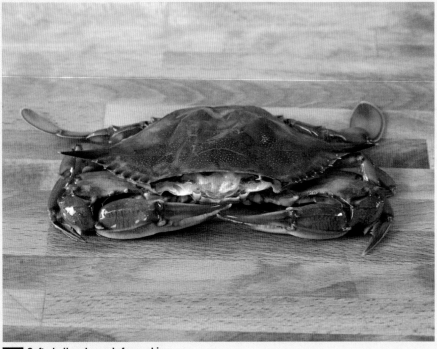

9 Soft-shell crab, ready for cooking.

IDENTIFYING MALE AND FEMALE CRABS

Female crabs are generally smaller than males and will have a broad apron (the large flap of shell on the belly side). On an immature female (known as a *sally* or *she-crab*) the apron will be triangular in shape. On a mature female (known as a sook), the apron will be rounded with a pointed tip. The T-shaped male's apron will be narrow and pointy. There are various state regulations to limit the harvest of females to ensure the health of stocks.

The male crab, with its narrow, pointed apron is on the left; the female crab with its rounded apron is on the right.

HIKING THE NOTORIOUSLY DIFFICULT WEST COAST TRAIL ON THE WEST COAST OF VANCOUVER ISLAND WILL OPEN ANYONE'S EYES TO THE AMAZING ABUNDANCE OF LIFE ALONG THOSE SHORES—SOURCE OF MUCH OF THE FOOD SERVED AT SOOKE HARBOUR HOUSE.

SINCLAIR PHILIP:
OWNER OF SOOKE HARBOUR HOUSE, VANCOUVER ISLAND, BRITISH COLUMBIA, CANADA

Although I haven't yet had the pleasure of visiting Sooke Harbour House, it has been long been a dream of mine to get there, especially after meeting owner Sinclair Philip in Seattle at a food conference. In 1979 Fréderique and Sinclair Philip purchased Sooke Harbour House, originally built in 1929 with just five small guestrooms. The inn now has twenty-eight rooms and a top-rated restaurant where the menu changes daily, serving only the freshest local ingredients including salad greens and more than 200 herbs that are grown in their own kitchen gardens. The restaurant specializes in wild seafood, generally served the very day it is caught by local fishers, and has introduced its customers to the many kinds of delicious sea vegetables.

YOUR MENU EMPHASIZES WILD SEAFOOD. WHAT ARE SOME OF THE SPECIES THAT YOU CATCH AND IN WHAT SEASON?
We have far more difficulty procuring most types of seafood than we did thirty years ago. At that time, we had wide varieties of seafood at low cost and the fish that we received was much fresher because so much of it came in live. Generally, we serve more fish in the summer months and more shellfish in the winter months.

WHAT WAS THE AVAILABILITY OF SEAFOOD LIKE IN THE EARLY DAYS OF THE RESTAURANT (1980S)?
Back then, we were able to get a wide selection of fish and shellfish. We bought almost everything locally from farmers and fishermen and about 30 percent of the food that came into our kitchen was alive, including giant Pacific octopus. We knew the vast majority of the fishermen and divers on a first-name basis and would often serve them in our restaurant dining room. The Rodd brothers would deliver northern abalone to our door for $2.00 a pound.

We would accompany geoduck divers like Les Tulloch to harvest them straight out of local waters and were perhaps the first in the region to buy pink swimming scallops. There was a big sea urchin fishery and we'd get live, green, purple, and red sea urchins delivered to their door as well as live sea cucumber, which we served frequently. We collected large numbers of marine snails including periwinkles, hornmouthed snails, and limpets and were able to buy excellent giant flying squid mantles not found since.

WHY DID THE SITUATION CHANGE?
Back then, a special C license allowed small boats to go out for short periods of time so they could bring fish and shellfish back alive. The fishermen would sell their bycatch to the inn, including all kinds of fish never seen today, such as sculpin, cabazon, and idiot rockfish. Sadly, today, the town of Sooke Harbour has only a small crab and small shrimp fishery after the small vessels were replaced by a fishing fleet of very large corporate ships.

*Fresh Pacific Northwest
wild salmon roe*

WHO DOES THE FISHING AND HOW—ARE THESE DIVERS, SMALL-SCALE FISHERMEN, OR MEMBERS OF YOUR OWN STAFF?

Thirty years ago, we had a number of small fishing vessels in our harbour. Now, more than 90 percent of our local fishermen are gone. Except for crab, shrimp, pink salmon, and albacore tuna boats, there are practically no small vessels left and far fewer fish and shellfish. These have been replaced by large draggers and very large fishing vessels that no longer sell in our town. The fish packing plant here closed down with the disappearance of the local fishery. We still have daily crab fishing boats, including my next-door neighbor, who operates a single boat.

DO YOU ALSO BUY SEAFOOD COMMERCIALLY?

One of our major suppliers is Finest at Sea in Victoria, which is an hour away from here by car. We also buy from Gordy Hohort, the Iron Maiden, and others, all comparatively small local suppliers.

----

*Sinclair Phillip, owner of Sooke
Harbour House, with local catch*

DO YOU SERVE ANY FARMED SEAFOOD? IF SO, WHAT KIND?

We do not serve farmed fish. The public here would not buy it, even from a chain. We do serve farmed mussels and oysters.

ARE THERE ANY SPECIES THAT YOU WISH CUSTOMERS WOULD RESPOND BETTER TO?

Our customers are generally happy with quite a wide variety of seafood and wish that we could offer more uncommon species that are no longer available because there is no fishery or because they are rare and endangered such as gooseneck barnacles and wild abalone.

HOW ABOUT GEODUCKS, RAZOR CLAMS, AND GOOSENECK BARNACLES—ALL PACIFIC NORTHWEST NATIVE SPECIES?

We often serve geoducks or piddock clams. There is no commercial razor clam industry open here at the moment. There was a commercial gooseneck barnacle fishery from 1978 to 1999 and they were an important traditional food of our First Nations. These days, there is no commercial fishery, but individuals collect them for their own consumption.

ARE THERE FISH THAT YOU CAN'T FIND ANYMORE?

We cannot get most of the fish that we purchased thirty years ago, either because those fisheries are not open or because there are no small boats left to fish for these species. A number of species are shipped out of the country and are never offered to us. Other species have become extinct. If you read David Suzuki's report, "Dragging Our Assets" (www.davidsuzuki.org), you will see that overfishing in our area has caused dramatic declines in species numbers and some extinctions. Even several species of salmon are now rarely available.

WHAT KIND OF SEA VEGETABLES DO YOU SERVE?

We serve a large variety of local sea vegetables such as dulse (*Palmaria palmata*), nori, laver or purple laver (*Porphyra*), tangle or kombu, and black seaweed (*Porphyra abbottae*)—an important food for the First Nations people. Our guests also enjoy bull kelp, sea lettuce (*Ulva spp., U. fenestrata, U. lactuca,* and others), small ribbon kelp (*Alaria nana*), and sugar kelp (*Laminaria saccharina*). The herring spawn on kelp (*komochi kombu* or *kazunoko kombu* in Japanese) we serve is herring roe fertilized on *Macrocystis*, or kelp—a major resource for Northwest Native people that is primarily exported to Japan. This sustainable food has been placed on Slow Food's Canadian Ark of Taste. We also serve sea samphire (also known as salty horn, *criste marine*, or *salicornia*), a delicious freshwater-estuary plant that is abundant in our region.

MATERIALS NEEDED:

Clean work surface

Pot of water

Bowl of cold water

Utility knife

Slicing knife

Meat mallet

Tray for the geoduck

CLEANING GEODUCK

The world's largest burrowing clam, the geoduck (pronounced "gooey-duck"), *Panopea abrupta*, gets its odd name from a Nisqually Native American term meaning "dig deep." It is native to the Pacific Northwest but is exported around the world.

The siphon, the main part that is eaten, protrudes from a pair of semi-open oval shells and has smooth, cream-colored flesh beneath the skin with a crunchy texture and strong flavor of the sea.

Geoducks are harvested individually by divers who use water jets to loosen the sand in which they burrow deeply. They are a delicacy in Asia, where they are cooked in Chinese and Korean cuisine and eaten raw in Japan as sashimi, called *mirugai* or *mirukuigai*. It is sometimes called *king clam*, for reasons that can easily be guessed, or as *elephant trunk clam*, a direct translation from Chinese.

Geoducks should be kept alive until ready to clean, which should be done as soon as possible after harvest. To store live geoducks, place them in a bucket and cover with a cool, damp cloth. Keep it in a cool location, out of direct sun. Do not immerse the geoducks in water or store in an airtight container or they will die.

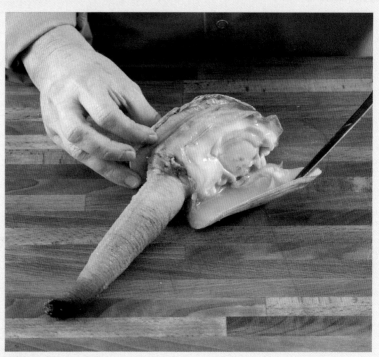

1 Bring a pot of water to boil and have ready a bowl of cold water. Rinse all sand from the geoducks. Scrape a knife along the inside of the shell to expose the viscera and open the shell.

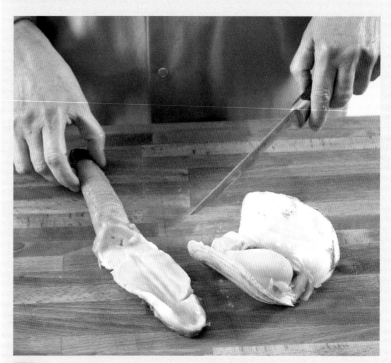

4 The edible portion of the geoduck is on the left. Discard the shell and viscera.

2 The mantle, the portion covering the viscera between the two shells, is edible. Insert the knife under the mantle to cut it away from the viscera.

3 Lift up the mantle. Use your knife to cut away the mantle, leaving it attached to the siphon, the tubelike protrusion of the geoduck.

5 To peel the tough skin off the siphon and mantle, place the geoduck in boiling water for about 45 seconds. Peel the skin starting with the body and continuing off the end of the siphon.

6 Peel the skin from the geoduck.

7 Cut between the more tender mantle and the tougher siphon.

8 Split the siphon by inserting a knife or scissors into it, cutting the siphon in two lengthwise. Wash the siphon, removing all traces of sand and grit.

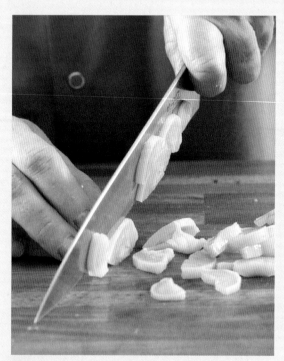

9 Slice the siphon meat thinly. To tenderize for sautéing, slice thinly at an angle and pound gently with the smooth side of a meat mallet (as for abalone, see "Cleaning Live Abalone"). It is not necessary to pound the mantle portion, which is more tender than the siphon.

10 Geoduck with sliced siphon, mantle, and shell portion.

MATERIALS NEEDED:

Large sink, bathtub, or ice chest

Water

Salt

Large pot

Lemon

Crawfish boil (or crab boil, if desired)

Wire basket (optional)

Platter for serving

Clean work surface

Container for the meat

Container for the shells

PREPARING CRAWFISH

Crawfish (or crayfish) are small freshwater crustaceans that look like miniature lobsters. In North America, the most important farmed species is the red swamp crawfish, *Procambarus clarkii*, from southern Louisiana. They are favorites in Creole and Cajun cooking, most often boiled in a big pot of spiced broth. Locals save the best for last: sucking out the tasty juices from the head, which contains the flavorful fat. The vast majority of these crawfish are trapped in the wild and farmed as a rotating crop with rice. Many other types of crawfish have harder shells. The delectable European crawfish, *Astacus astacus*, is found throughout Europe and is an essential ingredient for the classical French Sauce Nantua that often tops the ultra-light creamy pike fish dumplings, *quenelle de brochet*.

Because crawfish live in muddy waters, it is best to purge or clean their insides before cooking them. Pour the crawfish into a large sink, bathtub, or ice chest. Add enough water to just cover the crawfish and then mix with several spoonfuls of salt, mixing well, then rinse the crawfish. Keep the crawfish in a cool place exposed to the air until you're ready to start cooking.

To get started, cook the crawfish: Bring a large pot filled halfway with salted water to a boil. Cut a lemon in two, squeeze the juice into the water, then add the lemon rinds to the pot. Add crawfish boil (or crab boil if desired) to taste. Bring to the boil over high heat. Reduce the heat and simmer 10 minutes so the spice flavor is incorporated, then turn back to high and boil 2 to 3 minutes so the spices mix well with the water. Place the crawfish in a wire basket (ideally) and add them to the seasoned boiling water. Bring the water back to boil over high heat. Boil the crawfish for 5 minutes or until they are bright red. Turn off the heat, cover, and allow the crawfish to soak for about 20 minutes so they'll absorb the spice flavor from the broth. Lift crawfish from the broth with the wire basket and serve.

1 Fresh Louisiana crawfish (shown here) are in season from late February to mid-May.

2 To remove the delicious tail meat from cooked crawfish, grasp the crawfish by its head, with your nonwriting hand.

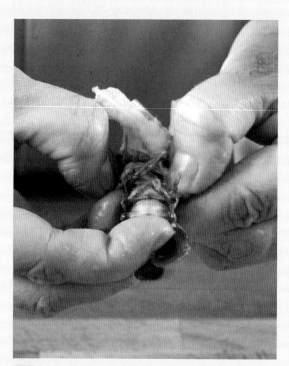

5 To remove the crawfish tail shell, hold it in your hand, inner side facing up.

6 Crack the shell lengthwise down the back then begin pulling off the shell, taking care to keep the tender tail meat intact.

3 Grasp the tail with your other hand and gently squeeze the tail end of the body close to where it attached to the main body shell. Gently twist the tail end while applying pressure.

4 The meaty tail twists out of the shell with some of the tasty fat from inside the crawfish on its end. Note that the Cajun people save the juicy, fatty heads for last, sucking the juices out of them. The claws contain very small amounts of meat.

7 Remove the tail shell. To remove the final tail portion inside the five fan-shaped final tail segments, crack them backward and twist them gently back and forth. Pull the entire tail meat out of the shell. Note the pointy end—this extra-colorful part will tend to break off if the crawfish isn't handled gently.

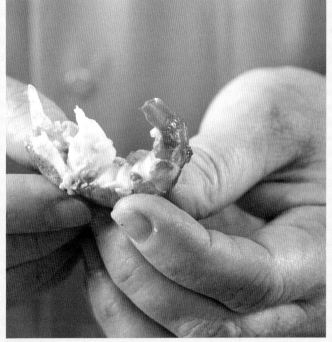

8 Crawfish tail meat, ready to eat.

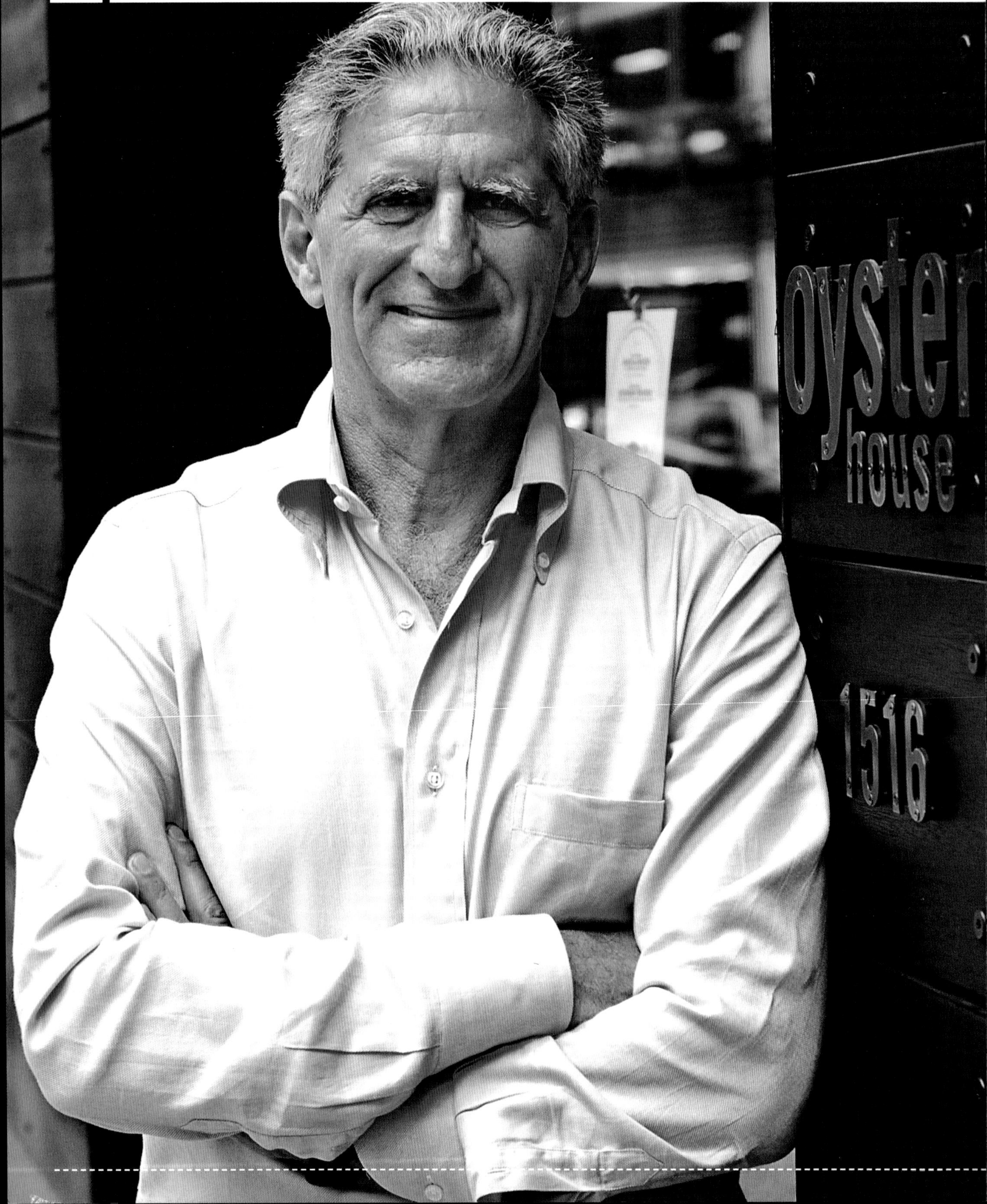
oyster
house
1516

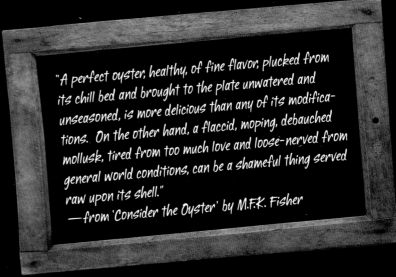

"A perfect oyster, healthy, of fine flavor, plucked from its chill bed and brought to the plate unwatered and unseasoned, is more delicious than any of its modifications. On the other hand, a flaccid, moping, debauched mollusk, tired from too much love and loose-nerved from general world conditions, can be a shameful thing served raw upon its shell."
—from 'Consider the Oyster' by M.F.K. Fisher

DAVID MINK:
FOUNDER OF THE OYSTER HOUSE, PHILADELPHIA, PENNSYLVANIA

To learn more about buying oysters, we spoke to an oyster expert, David Mink, a second-generation oyster monger and founder in 1976 of Philadelphia's Sansom Street Oyster House. In 1947, Mink's family bought the original Kelly's on Mole Street, a traditional Philadelphia oyster bar open since 1901. Mink sold the Sansom Street Oyster House in 2000 and retired— for a few years. In 2008, his son, Sam, bought back the business and re-opened it as the Oyster House with the help of his father.

The Mink family emphasizes East Coast oysters from the United States and Canada in its newly renovated modern oyster bar with displays of the family's collection of antique and unusual oyster plates gracing the walls. Almost all the oysters sold at the Oyster House are the same species, *Crassostrea virginica*, native to the North American Atlantic coast, though each type of oyster has a different flavor profile and texture according to water and weather conditions.

Founder David Mink at the entrance to the Oyster House, Philadelphia

WHAT'S THE BEST WAY TO CHOOSE AN OYSTER?
Tap the oyster: it should have a firm, solid sound. If you hear something that sounds like teeth rattling, the oyster is no good. An oyster should have weight in your hands; that's the water it contains. Oysters are hermaphroditic, each containing both sets of sex organs. Their sex changes depending on the age of the oyster. Look at the rings on an oyster shell. The oyster grows a new ring about once a year and in that time grows about one inch.

FROM WHOM DO YOU BUY YOUR OYSTERS?
We buy our oysters from a wholesaler, though I used to buy direct from a lot of people. Just to show how market has changed, in the late 1970s, I would buy *Bélons* [European Flats] from Maine, because we summered up there. I hooked up with a guy in Damariscotta. He would put my oysters on a bus and twelve hours later we would get them. I was first to bring Bélons into Philadelphia. Now, the trucks come down from Maine two to three times a week.

Shucking oysters at the Oyster House

DO YOU EVER BUY OYSTERS IN RETAIL MARKETS?

Even here, we don't shuck every oyster we sell. Those that we plan to cook, we buy already shucked in one-gallon tins. Similar oysters packed in jars and sealed at the source are available in retail markets. I do now see more abundant harvest dating of product, which is critical.

HOW DO YOU BUY AND STORE YOUR OYSTERS?

Our oysters come in net bags or wax boxes and include a tag with the name of the harvester, the date harvested, the date shipped, and the location of the bed. We keep our oysters in a special walk-in refrigerator at a relatively warm 40°F (4°C) temperature. Today, oysters are available year-round, though not all types are available every month. Having a lot of ice on hand is really important.

DO YOU PREFER COLD-WATER OR WARM-WATER OYSTERS?

I have a personal preference for cold water oysters. The flavor is pretty intense, the meat is very firm, and relatively small. At the Oyster House, we serve mostly cold-water oysters partly because they are safer than oysters from the Gulf [of Mexico] Coast [a warm-water region]. A natural occurring micro-organism, *Vibreo vulnificus*, occurs naturally in warm waters and can cause severe illness or even death for those with compromised immune systems who eat the oysters raw.

DO YOU HAVE ANY UNIQUE ITEMS ON YOUR MENU?

In the old days, I used to seek out oyster people wherever we traveled. When I visited Westcott Bay in Washington State's San Juan Islands, I met Bill Webb, a marine biologist who developed a triploid oyster, which doesn't spawn in water. He and his wife, Doree, came up with the idea for gourmet oysters after seeing scallops grown in lantern nets in Japan. When an oyster goes into its reproductive cycle, its composition changes and the meat gets mushy, leading to the old adage of not eating oysters in months containing the letter R. This didn't happen to triploid oysters, which reproduced asexually.

DO YOU SERVE EUROPEAN FLAT OYSTERS?

Yes. *Ostrea edulis* are often mistakenly called Bélons (only oysters harvested from the Bélon River in the French province of Brittany are entitled to that name) from Eastern Canada. These oysters are very fragile and can die quickly, so packers have learned to ship them differently. Distributors now ship them closed with rubber bands, well-side down, in trademark orange crates. If the oysters do open their shells, they don't lose their juices and deteriorate so they live longer.

HOW DO YOU SERVE YOUR OYSTERS?

Our experienced shuckers open every oyster to order while doing their best to keep the oysters whole and free of shell debris. We serve freshly-shucked oysters on crushed ice to keep them as cold as possible, partly because of food safety but mostly because they taste better.

WHAT'S THE MOST POPULAR OYSTER YOU SERVE?

The most common oyster available consistently throughout my forty-year career in the oyster business comes from Long Island, the most important source of oysters in the Mid-Atlantic region. They are commonly known as Bluepoints, but oysters now have appellations, like wine. It used to be that any oyster out of Long Island Sound was known as a Bluepoint [one word]. The original Bluepoints were robust wild oysters from the waters off the small town of Blue Point [two words] on Long Island's Great South Bay. By the early nineteenth century, those oysters were already disappearing because of overharvesting for the voracious New York City oyster market and because of pollution. The Bluepoint name then migrated to any oyster harvested from Long Island Sound. Chris Quartuccio, of Blue Island Oyster Farm, is now cultivating Bluepoint oysters in their original location near the Fire Island Inlet in the Great South Bay.

WHAT ARE THE DIFFERENCES BETWEEN WILD AND FARMED OYSTERS?

We have to be careful of how we define farming. Some oysters are farmed; some begin wild and are finished in a farm. There is a continuum between totally wild and very labor-intensive farmed oysters. An oyster can be natural and raised with minimum interference when you buy the oyster seed and spread it out in oyster beds, which adhere to rocks already set. In a more labor-intensive method, oysters are raised in nets above the ground and must be tended.

As the oyster grows, it must be taken from net, the dead ones removed, and the others moved to new containers so they have room to grow. These oysters grow above ground in a series of lantern-shaped nets, held up by buoys and weighted down, so water passes through the nets and the oysters filter out their food. The benefit of a cultured oyster is that it is raised intensely so you get a more consistent and cleaner oyster, minus pesky barnacles or the doubling commonly found in wild *Chincoteagues*, in which one oyster grows onto the shell of another.

DO YOU WORRY ABOUT POLUTION?

Coastal waters are a lot cleaner than they used to be. We have better [collective] awareness and we treat sewage better. As a result of cleaner water, we have more oysters in more areas. For years I had a sailboat, and only toward the end of my boating career did I start to see the bottom of the ground when in the bay, where it had always been cloudy.

OYSTER HISTORY 101

In the seventeenth century, the abundant oysters in New York Bay were one reason the Dutch bought Manhattan and Oyster (now Ellis) islands. The earliest oyster mongers in New York City sold their wares from street carts traditionally manned by African-Americans. The city's first tavern, Stadt Herbergh (City Tavern) was built in 1641 and contained a basement that was the forerunner of nineteenth-century oyster cellars. Pearly-white oysters on the half shell were a favorite subject of Dutch still-life paintings, and oyster bars are as popular today as when the city was known as New Amsterdam. Between 1880 and 1910, New York's golden age of oysters, its local beds produced about 700 millions oysters a year and oysters were sold on every block of Manhattan from street carts, oyster cellars, and palatial restaurants.

To the north, in Boston, the Union Oyster House has been serving oysters since 1826 and features a semicircular oyster bar where more than 3,000 oysters are shucked daily. New Orleans's French Quarter boasts the Acme Oyster House, first opened in 1910 as the Acme Café and still shucking about 10,000 oysters every day. Wintzell's Oyster House, a landmark in Mobile, Alabama, was founded in 1938 and is famous for its "Oysters—fried, stewed, or nude."

In Europe, Moran's Oyster Cottage in Galway, Ireland, dates back almost 300 years and is run by the seventh generation of the Moran family. Wiltons restaurant and oyster bar in London received its first Royal Warrant in 1884 as Purveyor of Oysters to Queen Victoria. In Paris, Alsatian brasseries such as Bofinger, which dates from 1864, La Coupole, from the 1930s, and L'Écume St.-Honoré are oyster-central, especially for *Bélons*. In Sydney, the Boathouse on Blackwattle Bay specializes in Sydney rocks and shucks them in-house (Australian oysters are often preshucked for export).

MATERIALS NEEDED

Oyster knife

Container of crushed ice

Container of cold water

Folded clean towel, preferably thick terry

Large cutting board

Oyster shucking glove to protect hands from stabs (optional but recommended, especially for novices), available left- or right-handed and used on your non-shucking hand

Special oyster plate for serving oysters or large serving plate filled with crushed ice

Accompaniments for oysters: lemon, mignonette sauce

SHUCKING OYSTERS

Oysters are saltwater bivalve mollusks that may be wild or farm-raised and everything between that feed by opening their shells and pumping huge amounts of seawater through their gills to filter out the plankton and other organisms they feed on, so oyster are beneficial for the environment. Oysters develop differences of appearance, shell and meat texture, and flavor depending on water conditions. Wild oysters from cold water have the most complex flavor, because cold water slows down their growth. Oysters live about twelve years, though most are harvested at about three years. An oyster that takes five years to grow to maturity on Cape Cod reaches full size in just three years in the Gulf of Mexico. Because an oyster's shell is filled with seawater, it can survive for long periods of time without having to open its shells, especially in winter months.

Oysters grow to fit their habitat, so slower-growing northern oysters are more regular, which makes them popular for serving on the half-shell. Wild oysters spawn in summer and are edible but tend to be flabby and insipid. Though farm-raised oysters are available year-round, oysters are at their best in winter. Because oysters filter so much seawater through their system, they are high in minerals such as iron, potassium, and zinc and are a good source of low-fat protein, making them a rare healthy indulgence. From ancient Rome to today, people have eaten oysters as a sexual stimulant. Two ancient aphrodisiacs, oysters and pine nuts, are high in zinc, which is necessary for sperm production.

METHOD ONE: OPENING OYSTERS FROM THE BACK

1 Have ready washed oysters in their shells on ice, preferably crushed, to keep them cold, an oyster knife, a container of clean water, a folded kitchen towel, preferably terry cloth, and crushed ice for serving a platter of freshly opened oysters.

2 Rinse the oyster in water.

3 Position the oyster with its cup side down on a clean towel, preferably terry cloth to better hold it in place, with the tip facing your writing hand. Locate the inner curve of the oyster just past the point.

4 Insert the tip of the knife into the back end of the oyster shell (shown here, Long Island oyster), pointed downward to avoid cutting the oyster meat. Using your body weight, press your palm down to hold the oyster in place while keeping your thumb at a 90-degree angle to the knife.

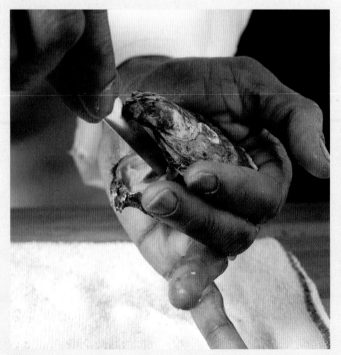

7 Once the shell is open, switch the knife position angling upward.

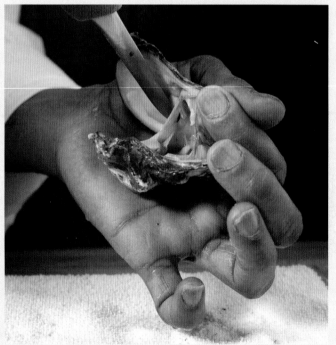

8 Scrape away the oyster meat from the top shell, ideally without cutting into the oyster itself.

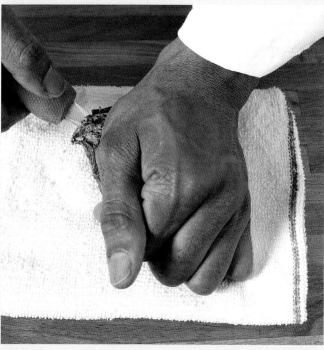

5 Slide and push the oyster knife farther into the shell using your palm to keep the oyster shell firmly in place.

6 Pop the shell open by twisting the knife toward the inside of the curve.

9 Oyster meat scraped cleanly away from the top shell.

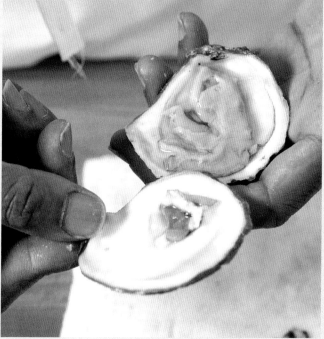

10 Pull up and twist off the top shell, leaving the oyster attached to the bottom shell.

11 Using the knife, pull up the oyster from its bed (it is still attached underneath to the shell) and gently scrape away any remaining shell debris from the shell.

12 Shelled oyster ready to be removed from its bottom shell.

13 Cut the oyster from the bottom shell by scraping toward the shell, not toward the oyster. While shucking, start a platter of the opened oysters on a bed of crushed ice, keeping them icy cold.

FIXING A SLIP OF THE KNIFE

If you cut into the oyster meat (see the dark spot at center), there's a solution: Using your knife, flip the oyster over to hide the cut side underneath. Voila—the oyster is "sunny-side up."

METHOD TWO: OPENING OYSTERS FROM THE HINGE

When I asked the expert shucker at Philadelphia's Oyster House how he knows which end to open the oyster from, he told me that each one will tell you the best way to open it. I suppose after spending twelve years doing nothing but shucking oysters for my job, I'd be able to tell too!

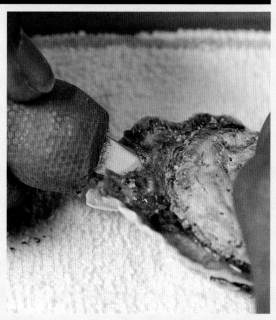

1 Some oysters are best opened from their hinge, especially this irregularly shaped Choptank. These oysters often have a brittle shell edge which may break off (as shown here).

2 Insert the tip of the knife into the hinge just past the point and toward the inside of the curve, wiggling and pushing the knife until it penetrates.

3 Pull off the top shell and scrape the oyster away from the top shell as in "Method One: Opening Oysters from the Back". Clean the oyster of debris as shown in step 11 in Method One.

4 Choptank oyster.

RESOURCES

CONTRIBUTORS

JANET AMATEAU
Owner, Tradescàntia Terrace Restaurant, 808-536-2148
www.pinedabar.com
Tradescantia, owned by Janet Amateau, is in Pineda de Mar, Spain, near Barcelona. The restaurant has an eclectic menu emphasizing traditional and creative Mediterranean food served on a garden terrace facing the sea with live jazz and bluegrass at night.

VELIA DE ANGELIS
Chef, cooking teacher, co-owner of La Champagneria
La Champagneria, Orvieto, Italy
0763 344102,
info@champagneria-orvieto.com
La Champagneria is a champagne bar in the heart of Orvieto, Italy serving appetizers prepared by de Angelis accompanied by a wide selection of champagnes.
www.champagneria-orvieto.com

Velia's Cooking Style,
Monterubiaglio (TR), Italy
0039 338 94 63 464
info@veliascookingstyle.com
www.veliascookingstyle.com/home.htm
Velia's Cooking Style is run by Chef Velia de Angelis with cooking classes in Umbria and an annual U.S. cooking tour.

CESARE CASELLA
Dean Italian Culinary Academy, owner of Salumeria Rosi, author,
www.salumeriarosi.com
Chef Cesare Casella's Salumeria Rosi is a small, neighborhood salumi shop and restaurant in New York City's Upper West Side, offering a wide variety of traditional Italian cured meats for dining or take-out.

SAMUEL D'ANGELO
Owner, Samuels and Son Seafood
www.samuelsandsonseafood.com
Samuels and Son Seafood is a distribution company is located at the Philadelphia Seafood Distribution Center in a 70,000 square foot (6,500 square meter) state-of-the-art facility.

SHEILA AND MIKE DASSATT
DownEast Lobstermen's Association
www.downeastlobstermen.org
The DownEast Lobstermen's Association (DELA) represents Maine fishermen and their families to sustain traditional lobstering as it has been upheld for generations.

AGLAIA KREMEZI
Greek culinary authority, journalist, and author, Kea Artisanale
www.keartisanal.com
Aglaia Kremezi hosts small groups for six-day programs on the Cycladic island of Kea with hands-on cooking classes, wine tasting, and exploration of the island's beaches, villages, and cultural sites.

LANCE FORMAN
H. Forman and Son
www.formans.co.uk
London's famed fish smokehouse, established in 1905, produces top quality smoked salmon, speciality fish, and bespoke prepared food. Forman's Fish Island, a restaurant and bar specializing in cured salmon and seasonal British foods, is located in the closest venue to the 2012 Olympic Stadium.

CHRIS LEFTWICH
Billingsgate Market
www.billingsgate-market.org.uk
Billingsgate Market is London's historic fish market.
www.seafoodtraining.org
Seafood School at Billingsgate Market offers free fish preparation and cookery courses for local schools, community, and voluntary groups at the Billingsgate Market, London.

ZARELA MARTINEZ
Zarela Restaurant, New York City
www.zarela.com/restaurant
For 22 years, Zarela Restaurant has been revolutionizing the way Americans perceive Mexican food at Zarela Martinez's Manhattan restaurant.

JEMMA MCCOWEN
Marketing Specialist, Cleanseas
www.cleanseas.com.au
Cleanseas is an Australian company that raises Kingfish, Mulloway, and Southern Bluefin Tuna sustainably.

MICHAEL MCNICHOLAS
Uoriki Fresh
www.minus76.com
A supplier of Japanese superfrozen tuna, Uoriki Fresh, a subsidiary of Mitsubishi, provides unique ultra deep freezing technology and frozen supply chain infrastructure.

DAVID MINK
Owner, the Oyster House, Philadelphia, PA
215-567-7683
www.oysterhousephilly.com
Serving Philadelphians fresh seafood at reasonable prices using local ingredients whenever possible and presenting Oyster House classics with a modern fresh taste.

SANDY NGUYEN
Coastal Communities Consulting
ccc-nola.org/about.html
A non-profit organization founded by Sandy Nguyen, Coastal Communities Consulting provides a holistic approach to economic development for Louisiana's entrepreneurs and their families.

SINCLAIR PHILIP
Sooke Harbour House
Sooke, BC, Canada
250-642-3421
www.sookeharbourhouse.com
Sooke Harbour House is a restaurant and inn on Vancouver Island specializing in locally sourced and harvested foods and seafood.

JAY SILVER
Fishmonger, George's Dreshertown Shop n Bag
Dresher, PA 19025
215-628-8055
www.georgesmarket.com
Locally owned supermarket with well-stocked fish department and knowledgeable fishmongers near Philadelphia.

FRANK SYDOW
General Manager, Hotel Jirahara, Barquisimeto, Venezuela
www.jiraharahotel.com.ve

BROOKS TAKENAKA
Assistant General Manager, United Fishing Agency (the Honolulu Fish Auction)
Honolulu, HI 96817
Hawaii Seafood Council
www.hawaii-seafood.org
Hawaii Seafood Buyer's Guide

NATALIE WEBSTER
Co-founder, American Albacore Fishing Association
www.americanalbacore.com
The American Albacore Fishing Association is a non-profit organization representing commercial pole and troll tuna vessels.

BOOKS

CEVICHE!
Seafood, Salads and Cocktails with a Latino Twist
Chef Guillermo Pernot with Aliza Green, Running Press, 2002, James Beard award-winner.

EATING WELL:
A Guide to the Foods of the Pacific Northwest
John Doerper
Pacific Search Press, 1984
An unassuming book with no photos but good descriptions and background for seafood species native to the Pacific Northwest such as geoduck, razor clam, and abalone.

THE ENCYCLOPEDIA OF FISH COOKERY
A.J. McClane
Holt, Rinehart and Winston, 1977
A classic book that is more than thirty years old but still full of valuable information, gorgeous photos, and an international viewpoint.

FIELD GUIDE TO SEAFOOD
Aliza Green, Quirk Books, 2007
Pocket guide to fish and shellfish species worldwide from the cook's point of view with yields, flavor affinities, cooking methods, and species names in 15 to 20 languages for each listing.

THE FOUNDING FISH
John McPhee, Farar, Straus, & Giroux, 2002
Explores the place of shad in American history, culture, and cuisine.

MEDITERRANEAN SEAFOOD
A Comprehensive Guide with Recipes
Alan Davidson, Ten Speed Press, 2002
Erudite descriptions of species with illustrations and traditional recipes.

NORTH ATLANTIC SEAFOOD
A Comprehensive Guide with Recipes
Alan Davidson, Ten Speed Press, 2002
Detailed desciptions of more than 100 species, with illustrations and their use in cuisine.

ON FOOD AND COOKING
Harold McGee, Scribner, 2004
www.curiouscook.com
Indespensible resource for anyone interested in the why of food. On his website, Curious Cook, McGee explores the science of food and cooking: where our foods come from, what they are and what they're made of, and how cooking transforms them.

PACIFIC NORTHWEST WINING AND DINING
Braiden Rex-Johnson
John Wiley & Sons, 2007
THE PIKE PLACE MARKET COOKBOOK
Braiden Rex-Johnson
Sasquatch Books, 2003
www.northwestwininganddining.com

THE RIVER COTTAGE FISH BOOK
Hugh Fearnley-Whittingstall and Nick Fisher
Bloomsbury, 2007
Excellent resource for understanding fish, cooking fish, and learning about British fish and seafood species from the famous River Cottage Restaurant and related businesses that have grown out of the restaurant.

SOURCING SEAFOOD:
A Professional's Guide to Procuring Ocean-friendly Fish and Shellfish, second edition
Seafood Choices Alliance, 2007, Silver Spring, MD 20910, 301-495-9570
www.seafoodchoices.org

FISHMONGER RESOURCES

COOKE AQUACULTURE
www.cookeaqua.com
New Brunswick, Canada salmon and trout aquaculture company committed to sustainability of the communities in which the company operates and the health of marine resources.

DRAGGING OUR ASSETS
www.davidsuzuki.org
www.davidsuzuki.org/publications/reports/2007/dragging-our-assets-toward-an-ecosystem-approach-to-bottom-trawling-in-canada
Report by the David Suzuki Foundation sustainable fisheries analyst Scott Wallace, offering recommendations to reduce the ecological impact of bottom trawling while maintaining access to fisheries resources.

ENVIRONMENTAL DEFENSE FUND
www.edf.org/documents/1980_pocket_seafood_selector.pdf
Pocket seafood selector

FANTE'S KITCHENWARE
www.fantes.com/seafood-tools
Truly has everyting when it comes to seafood tools and fish filleting knives.

FISH WATCH
www.nmfs.noaa.gov/fishwatch
U.S. seafood lists searchable by species. Accurate up-to-date information and seafood news.

GRANGE RESTAURANT
926 J Street
Sacramento, CA 95814
916-492-4450
www.grangesacramento.com
Chef Michael Tuohy's seasonally influenced restaurant adjacent to the Citizen's Hotel; Sacramento's showcase for the celebrated foods and wines of California.

KALUSTYAN'S
New York, NY 10016
212-685-3451
www.kalustyans.com
A landmark store carrying over 4,000 spices, herbs, legumes, condiments, and specialty foods from all over the world. A must for foodies visiting New York.

LA TIENDA
1325 Jamestown Road
Williamsburg, VA 23185
800-710-4304
www.latienda.com
Source for specialty foods imported from Spain.

LOCH DUART
www.lochduart.com
www.rspca.org.uk/freedomfood
Raises high-quality aquafarmed salmon in Scotland; the first salmon farm in the world to become a member of the RSPCA (Royal Society for the Prevention of Cruelty to Animals) Freedom Food's new salmon scheme.

MAGGIE BEER:
A Barossa Food Tradition
www.maggiebeer.com.au
Australian specialty foods created by South Australian cook, food author, restaurateur, and food manufacturer Maggie Beer.

MARINE STEWARDSHIP COUNCIL
www.msc.org
A global organization working with fisheries, seafood companies, scientists, conservation groups, and the public to promote the best environmental choice in seafood, working with partners (such as Samuels and Son Seafood) to encourage sustainable fishing practices.

MONTEREY BAY AQUARIUM
www.montereybayaquarium.org
Seafood Watch pocket guides organized by region.

MORTY THE KNIFE MAN
www.mortytheknifeman.com
Seafood tools used by professionals.

UNITED NATIONS FOOD AND AGRICULTURE ORGANIZATION
www.fao.org/docrep/005/v9878e/v9878e00.htm
Code of Conduct for Responsible Fisheries

UNIVERSITY OF CALIFORNIA, DAVIS
http://seafood.ucdavis.edu/consumer.html
Seafood resources page with links to many useful information and how-to sites.

WORSHIPFUL COMPANY OF FISHMONGERS'
www.fishhall.org.uk
One of the most ancient of the London City Guilds, with an unbroken existence of more than 700 years. Edward I granted them their first Charter in 1272 providing that no fish could be sold in London except by the "Mistery of Fishmongers."

INDEX

ACKNOWLEDGMENTS

So many generous people helped me research and write this book, sharing their invaluable experience, tips, and titbits. My special thanks to Samuel D'Angelo, owner of Samuels and Son Seafood, who acted as industry advisor for the book, allowing us access to Samuels amongst all the busy work of receiving, processing, packing, and shipping that goes on every day. Joe Lasprogata, the company's director of purchasing, worked closely with us to produce the techniques in the book, making sure that we had all the beautiful product we needed, whether geoduck from the Pacific Northwest, rouget from the Mediterranean, or crawfish from Louisiana, even when we showed up on the busiest week of the year—just before Mother's Day! Thanks to Anthony D'Angelo for showing me the best way to prepare abalone. Thanks to our expert cutters at Samuels: Pham Mung and Hang Nguyen. Many thanks to Ameen Lawrence, proud and skillful oyster shucker at The Oyster House.

Of course, none of this would have happened without the cheerful and careful work of the book's editor, Rochelle Bourgault. We've had a lot of fun and groans snagging sea-puns and sayings—that list is growing longer every day! Many thanks to Clare Pelino, of ProLiterary Agency, for finding Quarry Books. And, thanks to Steve Legato, who takes the most beautiful food photographs with many dashes of offbeat humor.

Thanks to everyone I interviewed and everyone else I spoke to who helped me understand the incredibly complex seafood back story. Thanks to Jemma McCowen, of Cleanseas, for the great contacts through her network of international seafood experts. Thanks to Hayley MatsonMathes, co-author of the Hawaii Farmers Market Cookbook, for connecting me with Brooks Takenaka of United Fishing Agency, Honolulu. Thanks to Helene York, Director of Strategic Initiatives, Bon Appetit Management Company, for explaining what her company is doing to further seafood sustainability. Thanks to Paul Balthrop, Florida Department of Agriculture, Bureau of Seafood and Aquaculture Marketing, for teaching me about Florida seafood.

Special thanks to everyone who contributed recipes: Michael Tuohy, chef of Grange Restaurant, Sacramento, Braiden Rex-Johnson, Seattle food writer, Cesare Casella of Salumeria Rosi, chef-author Zarela Martinez, New York City, Sam Mink of the Oyster House, Philadelphia, Moon Krapugthong of Mango Moon Restaurant, Philadelphia, Maggie Beer of Maggie Beer, South Australian cook, author, restaurateur and food manufacturer, Janet Amateau of Restaurant Tradescantia, near Barcelona, Philip Sinclair of Sooke Harbour House on Vancouver Island, Sandy Nguyen of Coastal Communities Consulting in New Orleans, Amy Riolo, chef and consultant in Washington, DC, Velia de Angelia of Velia's Cooking Style, Umbria, Italy, Chef David Anderson of Portola Restaurant & Café at the Monterey Bay Aquarium, and Aglaia Kremezi of Kea Artisanale, Kea, Greece.

ABOUT THE AUTHOR

Aliza Green, author, journalist, and influential chef, has been a fish lover her whole life. A lifetime of seafood memories include alderwood planked wild salmon on Blake Island near Seattle, Washington, paella studded with bite-size octopus at Los Caracoles in Barcelona, Spain, and fresh-caught rouget (red mullet) cooked over a wild fennelwood fire on the island of Corsica. She is the author of ten successful cookbooks on subjects ranging from beans to baking. *The Fishmonger's Apprentice* is her third book about seafood. Green won the coveted James Beard award for co-authoring *¡Ceviche!: Seafood, Salads, and Cocktails With a Latino Twist* (Running Press, 2001) with chef Guillermo Pernot. Her *Field Guide to Seafood* (Quirk Books, 2007) is a compact encyclopedia of fish written from the cook's point of view that is a must at top restaurants and seafood markets.

To learn more about Green or to ask a culinary question, visit her website, www.alizagreen.com.

ABOUT THE PHOTOGRAPHER

Steve Legato's passion for food and photography has taken him all around the United States, though not quite the entire world—yet. His photography has been featured in *Art Culinaire*, the *New York Times*, *Bon Appetit*, *GQ*, *Wine Spectator*, *Food Arts*, *Travel & Leisure*, *Wine and Spirits*, *Philadelphia Magazine*, and *New Jersey Monthly*. He has photographed for more than thirty cookbooks, including *Ceviche!* by Guillermo Pernot, which won a James Beard Award in 2002, and *Nicholas: The Restaurant*, which was nominated for the 2010 IACP Cookbook award for photography. His favorite meal is sausage, egg, and cheese on a kaiser roll (in New York City).